Acknowledgement

This book is simply a small window into sharing my personal journey – it is to be read as an inner exploration of my soul expression through catharsis.

Explore how an allegorical story told over millennia fragmented my psyche - my soul - and how the continual suppression of the *real me* – desperately fighting to get out – left a deep sorrow within.

Hold the writings I share within your loving heart and without judgement. My hope is that in the process you will also give birth to your own truth.

Please read with an open mind and without expectations.

With All My Heart,

Alessandra Marion Jouberteix BBA

This book is based on a real journey and real events. Names, places and identifying details, occupations or professions, geographic facts (cities and streets) have been changed.

Contents

Published and Distributed by

Create Space

Editors: Cary Mangum and Brian Leslie Lewis

Researcher: Joseph "Joe" Panek

Teacher & Friend: GP Walsh

Graphic Design and Layout: Margaret Gomes

Illustrator: Katreena JoyAnne Jouberteix-Stoen

ISBN-13: 978-0692368442

ISBN-10: 0692368442

Printed in the United States of America

With Special Gratitude

To

Stephen Paul Sanfilippo

To You,

Becoming

Through Ariadne's Eyes

There is a sound

Not perceived by the ear,

A sound deeper

And louder than thunder.

The roar of the soul, listen...

ALESSANDRA MARION JOUBERTEIX BBA

There lived in the hills of Crete a monster called the Minotaur, a terrible beast with the body of a man and the head of a wild bull which the people, who were his prey, did not want to face.

So they built a massive house with uncountable rooms and winding ways that they called The Labyrinth, and tricked the Minotaur into going inside with no chance of leaving. But from that day forward, they were constantly reminded of his presence through his terrible bellowing as he vainly tried to escape and look for his next victim.

Greek Myth

The pain of the handcuffs along with the unbearable heat in the back of the police car put my brain into overload and sent me back in time to a little girl in Mexico –pulled out of bed, beaten, thrown under a kitchen table, freezing by the door winter's draft on a pile of urine-soaked burlap sacks. Sobbing, struggling to breathe and trying to comprehend my current nightmarish scenario, I realized my life was once again out of control. Millennium-old myths, societal laws, and forces beyond my control had conspired to knock me off my path into an earthly hell, where unbeknownst to me, I was to dwell for the next three years.

My choices were clear—I had to negotiate the Labyrinth, face the Minotaur –and win.

This is my story...

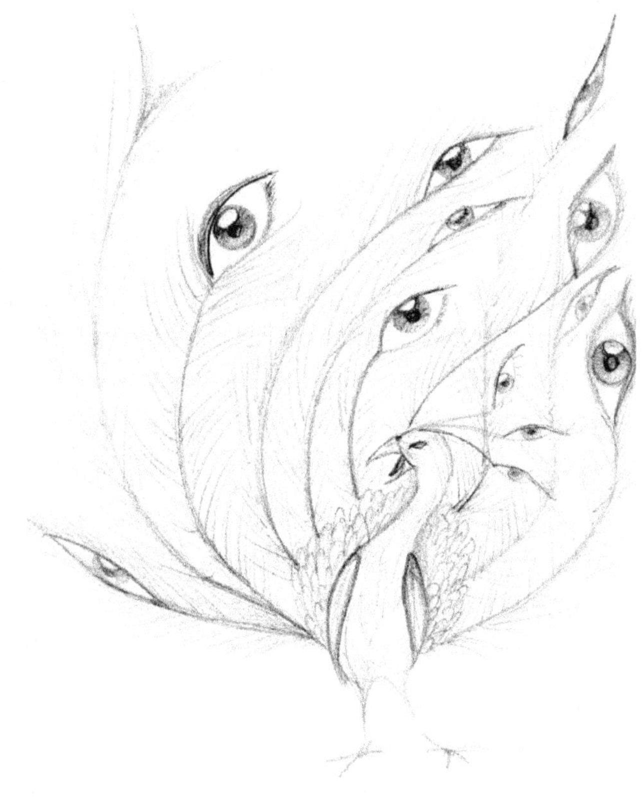

Chapter 1

MORPHING FATE

If one is to move the world, one must first move one's self.
-Socrates

Two decades ago I was in Mexico, homeless and with no-one to lean on. I was pregnant in a country where out-of-wedlock motherhood is close to a death sentence. It was likely that I would end up in prostitution to make ends meet or die of malnutrition. To my fortune, my only friend Chris made it possible for me to seek help in the United States by giving me contact information of one of his friends, a priest in the Lake Tahoe area.

I found new hope in my friend's words and the night before my flight to Reno, Nevada, I had called his friend and bluntly told him I was flying in the very next day and that I would appreciate any help. I told him I had a one-way ticket and $400 dollars in my pocket and regardless of his ability or willingness to help me, I was heading his way. He agreed to be at the airport at my arrival to fetch me. I did not share that I was two months pregnant.

My flight landed at 8:00 pm and I barely managed to find my way to the luggage area, given I did not speak a word of English. Yet, I was eager and hopeful to meet this stranger who had given me a glimpse into the possibility of a better life for myself and my unborn child.

Tense and anxious to meet him I arrived late only to find out that no one had shown up. No-one was there to greet me.

I sat and waited. I really did not know where I would go from here—the only connection I had in the country was this friend of a friend.

Was he ever going to show up? What was I to do if he never did? It was then that I realized the magnitude of my decision.

As I waited for the priest at the baggage claim area, my stories of childhood paraded in front of my eyes and I wondered if this meant the end of the line for me. And memories continued to flood my mind…

With my umbilical cord wrapped around my neck, my mother had given birth to me in 1968, on the side of the road in a cold afternoon in Del Rio, Texas. A few weeks later we would travel on a cargo ship across the ocean to accompany my father, an underground rebel fighting against Franco's Unitary Nationalism in the Basque area of southern France.

Our stay was cut short when he died in a train accident, most likely caused by one of many terrorist acts in that region. Alone and fearing for her safety, my mother returned to Mexico five years later. I was almost six years old.

She brought me to my maternal grandmother's house where I experienced the most glorious days of my life.

With grandmother I enjoyed nature and felt at one with the divine - chasing butterflies, marveling at tadpoles, lizards and fireflies; swimming with turtles at the water hole, looking for mushrooms in the horse corrals and playing in the mud. Many playful times were had at the river while grandmother washed clothes on the river rocks by the current.

There I enjoyed the fresh and clean smell of Earth and sat in the middle of cobblestone roads after the rainstorm, watching paper ships flow gently down the current. There I was free enjoying the hills, the sheep, and getting lost in the cornfields. Being in her garden and bathed while sitting on a huge volcanic rock by the well in my grandmother's garden, as hummingbirds flew by.

My heaven in that beautiful world ended dramatically and abruptly when at age of seven my mother once again took me to a Texas border town, El Paso, and left me with Mama Dee, a live-in daycare for working mothers. Her place was a living hell on earth. There, on a daily basis, I endured the most severe physical, emotional, and verbal abuse one could ever imagine.

My mother was supposed to fetch me at the end of the week and instead, she did not come back. And so I became an indentured servant to pay for my keep.

I was a feral child, put to work and any play was denied. Often I was hit with a whip, a water hose, or anything at arm's reach. Put to sleep under the kitchen table soaking in my own urine and sent to school without being allowed to change - to shame me so I would quit peeing in bed.

I had to perform the duties of an adult—without regard of the inclement weather conditions.

There, I learned how to work hard in a puritan way by doing laundry by hand, cleaning, ironing, washing cars, shoe polishing, and taking care of younger children. You name it -
I did it.

I became an adult at that young age and would not play again. I was denied the chance to experience child play and any possibility of joy, big or small just because...

Finally at age of 13 and tired of the daily abuse I ran away and found refuge at my Civics' teacher home.

Six months later my mother arrived to take me with her after being called by the Child Protective Services. When I refused to go with her she did not try to convince me otherwise. So, I tumbled from home to home for two years, until the age of 15 when a kind soul took financial responsibility for me and placed me in a girls Boarding School.

Six months later I received news that my mother was dying of cervical cancer at the young age of 33 and wanted to see me.

Even though I barely remember her presence in my life and I felt so much hate because of her abandonment, I also felt she was a human being with stage IV cancer and wanted to make peace. So I traveled to the north of Mexico to see her.

Shortly after my arrival I discovered that her sibling's intention was actually to get rid of her and that I was their vehicle to do it. They told me to take her to her home in the center of Mexico and that they would meet us in a week so we could all go to see an acupuncturist. It did not make sense to me that we did not go together, yet I was a child. I listened and traveled with my mother, carrying her. She was just a "bag of bones" and she was dying.

A week went by and nobody came. I waited another week and then sought monetary help from the neighbors for a bus fare to take her to my grandparent's place even though they did not want her there. They had told me to take care of her. I didn't have enough money to take care of myself!

So I stood my ground and decided to take her to my grandparents' house even though they had told me not to.

Their hate and resentment toward my mother was so great and I did not understand what she had done that was so unforgivable.

Being there I reconnected with friends from the short time I had lived there when I was six; and was often gone most of the time having fun. One of my aunts confronted me and demanded I take care of my mother but I refused insisting it was my grandparent's responsibility.

I left their home in Mexico after an altercation with my aunt and went back to the boarding school I was attending. A couple of months later I received a phone call that mother had died in her house in Mexico alone, aided only by her neighbors who had collected money for her funeral.

My grandparents who were deeply devoted Catholics, did not seem to have a grain of compassion in their hearts for their dying daughter. She had dragged herself out of their house leaving a trail of coagulated clots of blood in her path.

On my 18th birthday I left the boarding school and went out into the world with high hopes of developing a career and being "somebody".

And yet here I was, alone and pregnant, in a foreign country in the middle of winter, feeling utterly lost.

Chapter II

CORE WOUND

The unexamined life is not worth living.
-Socrates

Deeply immersed in my thoughts waiting for the priest, I sat waiting, pondering, wondering, full of uncertainty, and frightened to the core. What would I do? How much longer should I wait? Was I waiting in vain?

Finally, nearly 11 pm, almost three hours after my flight had arrived, I spotted him walking towards me. I was so relieved, hopeful and grateful that the winter storm had not deterred him from reaching me.

The priest took me to a family that kindly took me in and within few days I met sweet Anna, who suggested an exchange of babysitting skills for room and board. I eagerly moved in with her and her family.

When Anna found out about my pregnancy she helped me realize the predicament I was in. I was in a foreign country without being able to speak the language, sleeping in her walk-in closet – and she was on the verge of divorce. How was I to take care of the child I was expecting?

I was raised Catholic, which meant abortion was not an option. Terminating the pregnancy meant I would "burn in hell for eternity", literally. It also meant "losing my soul". Because Anna knew I would not go for an abortion, she suggested I consider giving the child up for adoption.

For a week, I went back and forth considering both hard propositions.

Either choice was a horrendous burden. I knew I would go to hell if I had an abortion. I also knew that I would not be able to give up my child, as I had personally experienced the pain of abandonment. Most importantly, I did not want my child to go through what I had gone through.

And so for me, the only choice was the lesser of two evils. Without the ability to take care of myself, how could I not follow in my mother 's footsteps? I chose to terminate the pregnancy and accept the loss of my soul rather than causing a lifelong chain of pain for abandoning my child.

I reflected on my mother and on how she was forced to leave me behind when she was unable to provide for me as a single mother. She had been labeled a whore for having an illegitimate child. Oh how painful it was to repeat the same story.

I reflected on the daily beatings and the voices of my caregivers telling me how stupid I was and how I would be a whore like my mother. The days of not being able to be a child like everyone else around me, and instead being constantly put to work. How my life seemed dictated at birth. Powerless.

My whole existence had been for service of others. My uniqueness had been disregarded and the use of fear and force had driven me into compliance - all individuality crushed. I did not wish the same for my child.

Chapter III

SAND CASTLES

Sometimes people do not want to hear the truth
because they do not want their illusions destroyed.
-Friedrich Nietzsche

Summer came and my friend Anna advised me to move to the San Francisco Bay Area where job opportunities were much better. Within a week I had a nanny job in a small nearby city with a Catholic family. I was full of hopes, given that I was getting a salary of $400 a month plus room and board.

So if I applied myself in the hope that someday I would save enough money to get a college degree, like I had always dreamed of.

Life was moving along well and weeks later I met a charming man. I shared openly with the family I was working with that Marc and I were friends and that we liked each other, but that I was not sure of having a boyfriend/ girlfriend relationship.

I wanted to take my time to get to know him. I also wanted the opportunity to date other people.

One Friday night, instead of cancelling a date I had with Marc, I invited him to come over for dinner while I babysat for the family at their last minute request.

At that time I had a hard time saying no to people and also lacked the social cues and fears which most people experience when dealing with strangers. Due to this, I did not tell the family about him coming over for dinner.

I did not see any harm in my decision given that I did not distrust Marc and felt safe and comfortable with him. He seemed a nice guy and I knew he worked for a prestigious corporation.

He came over and brought a thirty-two ounce beer with him to have with dinner. We had a pleasant time together while I took care of the baby. We ate, watched a movie, talked and then he left. We were only friends.

The following day the lady of the house was infuriated as she pointed at the empty glass bottle of beer on the countertop asking me the meaning of it. I did not understand. I explained that Marc had come for dinner and he had brought it with him. She was extremely offended with my behavior; and I was hurt and offended as well because in my eyes, I had done nothing wrong.

That incident changed how I related to them and I made the decision that from now on it would be best to keep my affairs private, outside their involvement.

Yet, it is a given that when you change one thing you change everything and very soon I was given a two-week notice to find another job.

Marc knew I did not have anywhere to go and feeling responsible for what had happened, he fetched me later that day.

And so, again I went into another house, thrown there seemingly at the whims of life.

I hardly knew Marc, and yet this abrupt way of moving into someone 's home was painfully familiar. I had lived with thirty families since the age of thirteen when I had ran away from my caregivers. I was a highly adaptable being and moving in with him to share the room he rented at his father's house was no challenge.

I felt so grateful to be there that I cooked and cleaned for everyone to show my appreciation. Everyone was nice, except one of the roommates, Janet, who called me a "stupid beaner", a demeaning term used for someone from Mexico. I was not sure why I caused her so much disgust but she really seemed to detest me.

One day I confronted her and when I asked her what I had done to deserve her mistreatment, she completely disregarded me and as she walked away, intending to shut the door in my face, my foot prevented her from doing so.

She screamed at Marc's father, saying *"get her out of my way or I will call immigration to fetch her and take her back to Mexico."*

I felt like I was going to pass out. Hell on earth was the last place I wanted to go to; so I backed off, trembling and weak to my knees. My passport had expired a couple of months earlier and she knew that.

Three months later, not able to handle the stress of constantly fearing the threat that immigration authorities would be coming for me to send me back to Mexico, I asked Marc to marry me.

He agreed and we got married. Soon after my traditional life as a housewife began. He was the breadwinner and I was to take care of everything for him. I was very grateful for his gesture to marry me even though he hardly knew me.

My Cinderella dream had finally come true. My prince had finally rescued me at last.

So, I thought.

THESEUS

&

THE MINOTAUR

While Athens was still only a small city there lived within its walls a man named Daedalus who was the most skillful worker in wood and stone and metal that had ever been known. It was he who taught the people how to build better houses and how to hang their doors on hinges and how to support the roofs with pillars and posts. He was the first to fasten things together with glue; he invented the plumb-line and the auger; and he showed seamen how to put up masts in their ships and how to rig the sails to them with ropes. He built a stone palace for AEgeus, the young king of Athens, and beautified the Temple of Athena, which stood on the great rocky hill in the middle of the city.

Daedalus had a nephew named Perdix whom he had taken when a boy to teach the trade of builder. But Perdix was a very apt learner, and soon surpassed his master in the knowledge of many things. His eyes were ever open to see what was going on about him, and he learned the lore of the fields and the woods. Walking one day by the sea, he picked up the backbone of a great fish, and from it he invented the saw. Seeing how a certain bird carved holes in the trunks of trees, he learned how to make and use the chisel. Then he invented the wheel which potters use in molding clay; and he made of a forked stick the first pair of compasses for drawing circles; and he studied out many other curious and useful things.

Daedalus was not pleased when he saw that the lad was so apt and wise, so ready to learn, and so eager to do.

"If he keeps on in this way," he murmured, "he will be a greater man than I; his name will be remembered, and mine will be forgotten."

Day after day, while at his work, Daedalus pondered over this matter, and soon his heart was filled with hatred towards young Perdix. One morning when the two were putting up an ornament on the outer wall of Athena's temple, Daedalus bade his nephew go out on a narrow scaffold which hung high over the edge of the rocky cliff whereon the temple stood. Then, when the lad obeyed, it was easy enough, with a blow of a hammer, to knock the scaffold from its fastenings.

Poor Perdix fell headlong through the air, and he would have been dashed in pieces upon the stones at the foot of the cliff had not kind Athena seen him and taken pity upon him. While he was yet whirling through mid-air she changed him into a partridge, and he flitted away to the hills to live forever in the woods and fields which he loved so well. And to this day, when summer breezes blow and the wild flowers bloom in meadow and glade, the voice of Perdix may still sometimes be heard, calling to his mate from among the grass and reeds or amid the leafy underwoods.

As for Daedalus, when the people of Athens heard of his dastardly deed, they were filled with grief and rage–grief for young Perdix, whom all had learned to love; rage towards the wicked uncle, who loved only himself. At first they were for punishing Daedalus with the death which he so richly deserved, but when they remembered what he had done to make their homes pleasanter and their lives easier, they allowed him to live; and yet they drove him out of Athens and bade him never return.

There was a ship in the harbor just ready to start on a voyage across the sea, and in it Daedalus embarked with all his precious tools and his young son Icarus. Day after day the little vessel sailed slowly southward, keeping the shore of the mainland always upon the right. It passed Troezen and the rocky coast of Argos, and then struck boldly out across the sea.

At last the famous Island of Crete was reached, and there Daedalus landed and made himself known; and the King of Crete, who had already heard of his wondrous skill, welcomed him to his kingdom, and gave him a home in his palace, and promised that he should be rewarded with great riches and honor if he would but stay and practice his craft there as he had done in Athens.

Now the name of the King of Crete was Minos. His grandfather, whose name was also Minos, was the son of Europa, a young princess whom a white bull, it was said, had brought on his back across the sea from distant Asia. This elder Minos had been accounted the wisest of men—so wise, indeed, that Zeus chose him to be one of the judges of the Lower World. The younger Minos was almost as wise as his grandfather; and he was brave and far-seeing and skilled as a ruler of men. He had made all the islands subject to his kingdom, and his ships sailed into every part of the world and brought back to Crete the riches of foreign lands. So it was not hard for him to persuade Daedalus to make his home with him and be the chief of his artisans.

And Daedalus built for King Minos a most wonderful palace with floors of marble and pillars of granite; and in the palace he set up golden statues which had tongues and could talk; and for splendor and beauty there was no other building in all the wide earth that could be compared with it.

There lived in those days among the hills of Crete a terrible monster called the Minotaur, the like of which has never been seen from that time until now. This creature, it was said, had the body of a man, but the face and head of a wild bull and the fierce nature of a mountain lion. The people of Crete would not have killed him if they could; for they thought that the Mighty Folk who lived with Zeus on the mountain top had sent him among them, and that these beings would be angry if anyone should take his life. He was the pest and terror of all the land. Where he was least expected, there he was sure to be; and almost every day some man, woman, or child was caught and devoured by him.

"You have done so many wonderful things," said the king to Daedalus, "can you not do something to rid the land of this Minotaur?"

"Shall I kill him?" asked Daedalus.

"Ah, no!" said the king. "That would only bring greater misfortunes upon us."

"I will build a house for him then," said Daedalus, "and you can keep him in it as a prisoner."

"But he may pine away and die if he is penned up in prison," said the king.

"He shall have plenty of room to roam about," said Daedalus; "and if you will only now and then feed one of your enemies to him, I promise you that he shall live and thrive."

So the wonderful artisan brought together his workmen, and they built a marvelous house with so many rooms in it and so many winding ways that no one who went far into it could ever find his way out again; and Daedalus called it the Labyrinth, and cunningly persuaded the Minotaur to go inside of it. The monster soon lost his way among the winding passages, but the sound of his terrible bellowing could be heard day and night as he wandered back and forth vainly trying to find some place to escape.

Not long after this it happened that Daedalus was guilty of a deed which angered the king very greatly; and had not Minos wished him to build other buildings for him, he would have put him to death and no doubt have served him right.

"Hitherto," said the king, "I have honored you for your skill and rewarded you for your labor. But now you shall be my slave and shall serve me without hire and without any word of praise."

Then he gave orders to the guards at the city gates that they should not let Daedalus pass out at any time, and he set soldiers to watch the ships that were in port so that he could not escape by sea. But although the wonderful artisan was thus held as a prisoner, he did not build any more buildings for King Minos; he spent his time in planning how he might regain his freedom.

"All my inventions," he said to his son Icarus, "have hitherto been made to please other people; now I will invent something to please myself."

So, all through the day he pretended to be planning some great work for the king, but every night he locked himself up in his chamber and wrought secretly by candle light. By and by he had made for himself a pair of strong wings, and for Icarus another pair of smaller ones; and then, one midnight, when everybody was asleep, the two went out to see if they could fly. They fastened the wings to their shoulders with wax, and then sprang up into the air. They could not fly very far at first, but they did so well that they felt sure of doing much better in time.

The next night Daedalus made some changes in the wings. He put on an extra strap or two; he took out a feather from one wing, and put a new feather into another; and then he and Icarus went out in the moonlight to try them again. They did finely this time. They flew up to the top of the king's palace, and then they sailed away over the walls of the city and alighted on the top of a hill. But they were not ready to undertake a long journey yet; and so, just before daybreak, they flew back home. Every fair night after that they practiced with their wings, and at the end of a month they felt as safe in the air as on the ground, and could skim over the hilltops like birds.

Early one morning; before King Minos had risen from his bed, they fastened on their wings, sprang into the air, and flew out of the city. Once fairly away from the island, they turned towards the west, for Daedalus had heard of an island named Sicily, which lay hundreds of miles away, and he had made up his mind to seek a new home there.

All went well for a time, and the two bold flyers sped swiftly over the sea, skimming along only a little above the waves, and helped on their way by the brisk east wind. Towards noon the sun shone very warm, and Daedalus called out to the boy who was a little behind and told him to keep his wings cool and not fly too high. But the boy was proud of his skill in flying, and as he looked up at the sun he thought how nice it would be to soar like it high above the clouds in the blue depths of the sky.

"At any rate," said he to himself, "I will go up a little higher. Perhaps I can see the horses which draw the sun car, and perhaps I shall catch sight of their driver, the mighty sun master himself."

So he flew up higher and higher, but his father who was in front did not see him. Pretty soon, however, the heat of the sun began to melt the wax with which the boy's wings were fastened. He felt himself sinking through the air; the wings had become loosened from his shoulders. He screamed to his father, but it was too late. Daedalus turned just in time to see Icarus fall headlong into the waves. The water was very deep there, and the skill of the wonderful artisan could not save his child. He could only look with sorrowing eyes at the unpitying sea, and fly on alone to distant Sicily. There, men say, he lived for many years, but he never did any great work, nor built anything half as marvelous as the Labyrinth of Crete. And the sea in which poor Icarus was drowned was called forever afterward by his name, the Icarian Sea.

Minos, king of Crete, had made war upon Athens. He had come with a great fleet of ships and an army, and had burned the merchant vessels in the harbor, and had overrun all the country and the coast even to Megara, which lies to the west. He had laid waste the fields and gardens round about Athens, had pitched his camp close to the walls, and had sent word to the Athenian rulers that on the morrow he would march into their city with fire and sword and would slay all their young men and would pull down all their houses, even to the Temple of Athena, which stood on the great hill above the town. Then AEgeus, the king of Athens, with the twelve elders who were his helpers, went out to see King Minos and to treat with him.

"O mighty king," they said, "what have we done that you should wish thus to destroy us from the earth?"

"O cowardly and shameless men," answered King Minos, "why do you ask this foolish question, since you can but know the cause of my wrath? I had an only son, Androgeos by name, and he was dearer to me than the hundred cities of Crete and the thousand islands of the sea over which I rule. Three years ago he came hither to take part in the games which you held in honor of Athena, whose temple you have built on yonder hilltop. You know how he overcame all your young men in the sports, and how your people honored him with song and dance and laurel crown. But when your king, this same AEgeus who stands before me now, saw how everybody ran after him and praised his valor, he was filled with envy and laid plans to kill him. Whether he caused armed men to waylay him on the road to Thebes, or whether as some say he sent him against a certain wild bull of your country to be slain by that beast, I know not; but you cannot deny that the young man's life was taken from him through the plotting of this AEgeus."

"But we do deny it–we do deny it!" cried the elders. "For at that very time our king was sojourning at Troezen on the other side of the Saronic Sea, and he knew nothing of the young prince's death. We ourselves managed the city's affairs while he was abroad, and we know whereof we speak. Androgeos was slain, not through the king's orders but by the king's nephews, who hoped to rouse your anger against AEgeus so that you would drive him from Athens and leave the kingdom to one of them."

"Will you swear that what you tell me is true?" said Minos.

"We will swear it," they said.

"Now then," said Minos, "you shall hear my decree. Athens has robbed me of my dearest treasure, a treasure that can never be restored to me; so, in return, I require from Athens, as tribute, that possession which is the dearest and most precious to her people; and it shall be destroyed cruelly as my son was destroyed."

"The condition is hard," said the elders, "but it is just. What is the tribute which you require?"

"Has the king a son?" asked Minos.

The face of King AEgeus lost all its color and he trembled as he thought of a little child then with its mother at Troezen, on the other side of the Saronic Sea. But the elders knew nothing about that child, and they answered:

"Alas, no! He has no son; but he has fifty nephews who are eating up his substance and longing for the time to come when one of them shall be king; and, as we have said, it was they who slew the young prince, Androgeos."

"I have naught to do with those fellows," said Minos; "you may deal with them as you like. But you ask 'what is the tribute that I require', and I will tell you. Every year when the springtime comes and the roses begin to bloom, you shall choose seven of your noblest youths and seven of your fairest maidens, and shall send them to me in a ship which your king shall provide. This is the tribute which you shall pay to me, Minos, king of Crete; and if you fail for a single time, or delay even a day, my soldiers shall tear down your walls and burn your city and put your men to the sword and sell your wives and children as slaves."

"We agree to all this, O King," said the elders; "for it is the least of two evils. But tell us now, what shall be the fate of the seven youths and the seven maidens?"

"In Crete," answered Minos, "there is a house called the Labyrinth, the like of which you have never seen. In it there are a thousand chambers and winding ways, and whosoever goes even a little way into them can never find his way out again. Into this house the seven youths and.the seven maidens shall be thrust, and they shall be left there–"

"To perish with hunger?" cried the elders.

"To be devoured by a monster whom men call the Minotaur," said Minos.

Then King AEgeus and the elders covered their faces and wept and went slowly back into the city to tell their people of the sad and terrible conditions upon which Athens could alone be saved.

"It is better that a few should perish than that the whole city should be destroyed," they said.

Years passed by. Every spring when the roses began to bloom seven youths and seven maidens were put on board of a black-sailed ship and sent to Crete to pay the tribute which King Minos required. In every house in Athens there was sorrow and dread, and the people lifted up their hands to Athena on the hilltop and cried out, "How long, O Queen of the Air, how long shall this thing be?"

In the meanwhile the little child at Troezen on the other side of the sea had grown to be a man. His name, Theseus, was in everybody's mouth, for he had done great deeds of daring; and at last he had come to Athens to find his father, King AEgeus, who had never heard whether he was alive or dead; and when the youth had made himself known, the king had welcomed him to his home and all the people were glad because so noble a prince had come to dwell among them and, in time, to rule over their city.

The springtime came again. The black-sailed ship was rigged for another voyage. The rude Cretan soldiers paraded the streets; and the herald of King Minos stood at the gates and shouted:

"Yet three days, O Athenians, and your tribute will be due and must be paid!"

Then in every street the doors of the houses were shut and no man went in or out, but every one sat silent with pale cheeks, and wondered whose lot it would be to be chosen this year. But the young prince, Theseus, did not understand; for he had not been told about the tribute.

"What is the meaning of all this?" he cried. "What right has a Cretan to demand tribute in Athens? And what is this tribute of which he speaks?"

Then AEgeus led him aside and with tears told him of the sad war with King Minos, and of the dreadful terms of peace. "Now, say no more," sobbed AEgeus, "it is better that a few should die even thus than that all should be destroyed."

"But I will say more," cried Theseus. "Athens shall not pay tribute to Crete. I myself will go with these youths and maidens, and I will slay the monster Minotaur, and defy King Minos himself upon his throne."

"Oh, do not be so rash!" said the king; "for no one who is thrust into the den of the Minotaur ever comes out again. Remember that you are the hope of Athens, and do not take this great risk upon yourself."

"Say you that I am the hope of Athens?" said Theseus. "Then how can I do otherwise than go?" And he began at once to make himself ready.

On the third day all the youths and maidens of the city were brought together in the market place, so that lots might be cast for those who were to be taken. Then two vessels of brass were brought and set before King AEgeus and the herald who had come from Crete. Into one vessel they placed as many balls as there were noble youths in the city, and into the other as many as there were maidens; and all the balls were white save only seven in each vessel, and those were black as ebony.

Then every maiden, without looking, reached her hand into one of the vessels and drew forth a ball, and those who took the black balls were borne away to the black ship, which lay in waiting by the shore. The young men also drew lots in like manner, but when six black balls had been drawn Theseus came quickly forward and said:

"Hold! Let no more balls be drawn. I will be the seventh youth to pay this tribute. Now let us go aboard the black ship and be off."

Then the people, and King AEgeus himself, went down to the shore to take leave of the young men and maidens, whom they had no hope of seeing again; and all but Theseus wept and were brokenhearted.

"I will come again, father," he said.

"I will hope that you may," said the old king. "If when this ship returns, I see a white sail spread above the black one, then I shall know that you are alive and well; but if I see only the black one, it will tell me that you have perished."

And now the vessel was loosed from its moorings, the north wind filled the sail, and the seven youths and seven maidens were borne away over the sea, towards the dreadful death which awaited them in far distant Crete.

At last the black ship reached the end of its voyage. The young people were set ashore, and a party of soldiers led them through the streets towards the prison, where they were to stay until the morrow. They did not weep nor cry out now, for they had outgrown their fears. But with paler faces and firm-set lips, they walked between the rows of Cretan houses, and looked neither to the right nor to the left. The windows and doors were full of people who were eager to see them.

"What a pity that such brave young men should be food for the Minotaur," said some.

"Ah, that maidens so beautiful should meet a fate so sad!" said others.

And now they passed close by the palace gate, and in it stood King Minos himself, and his daughter Ariadne, the fairest of the women of Crete.

"Indeed, those are noble young fellows!" said the king.

"Yes, too noble to feed the vile Minotaur," said Ariadne.

"The nobler, the better," said the king; "and yet none of them can compare with your lost brother Androgeos."

Ariadne said no more; and yet she thought that she had never seen anyone who looked so much like a hero as young Theseus. How tall he was, and how handsome! How proud his eye, and how firm his step! Surely there had never been his like in Crete.

All through that night Ariadne lay awake and thought of the matchless hero, and grieved that he should be doomed to perish; and then she began to lay plans for setting him free. At the earliest peep of day she arose, and while everybody else was asleep, she ran out of the palace and hurried to the prison. As she was the king's daughter, the jailer opened the door at her bidding and allowed her to go in. There sat the seven youths and the seven maidens on the ground, but they had not lost hope. She took

Theseus aside and whispered to him. She told him of a plan which she had made to save him; and Theseus promised her that, when he had slain the Minotaur, he would carry her away with him to Athens where she should live with him always. Then she gave him a sharp sword, and hid it underneath his cloak, telling him that with it alone could he hope to slay the Minotaur.

"And here is a ball of silken thread," she said. "As soon as you go into the Labyrinth where the monster is kept, fasten one end of the thread to the stone doorpost, and then unwind it as you go along. When you have slain the Minotaur, you have only to follow the thread and it will lead you back to the door. In the meanwhile I will see that your ship, is ready to sail, and then I will wait for you at the door of the Labyrinth."

Theseus thanked the beautiful princess and promised her again that if he should live to go back to Athens she should go with him and be his wife. Then with a prayer to Athena, Ariadne hastened away.

As soon as the sun was up the guards came to lead the young prisoners to the Labyrinth. They did not see the sword which Theseus had under his cloak, nor the tiny ball of silk which he held in his closed hand. They led the youths and maidens a long way into the Labyrinth, turning here and there, back and forth, a thousand different times, until it seemed certain that they could never find their way out again. Then the guards, by a secret passage which they alone knew, went out and left them, as they had left many others before, to wander about until they should be found by the terrible Minotaur.

"Stay close by me," said Theseus to his companions, "and with the help of Athena who dwells in her temple home in our own fair city, I will save you."

Then he drew his sword and stood in the narrow way before them; and they all lifted up their hands and prayed to Athena.

For hours they stood there, hearing no sound, and seeing nothing but the smooth, high walls on either side of the passage and the calm blue sky so high above them. Then the maidens sat down upon the ground and covered their faces and sobbed, and said:

"Oh, that he would come and put an end to our misery and our lives."

At last, late in the day, they heard a bellowing, low and faint as though far away. They listened and soon heard it again, a little louder and very fierce and dreadful.

"It is he! It is he!" cried Theseus; "and now for the fight!"

Then he shouted, so loudly that the walls of the Labyrinth answered back, and the sound was carried upward to the sky and outward to the rocks and cliffs of the mountains. The Minotaur heard him, and his bellowing grew louder and fiercer every moment.

"He is coming!" cried Theseus, and he ran forward to meet the beast. The seven maidens shrieked, but tried to stand up bravely and face their fate; and the six young men stood together with firm-set teeth and clinched fists, ready to fight to the last.

Soon the Minotaur came into view, rushing down the passage towards Theseus, and roaring most terribly. He was twice as tall as a man, and his head was like that of a bull with huge sharp horns and fiery eyes and a mouth as large as a lion's; but the young men could not see the lower part of his body for the cloud of dust which he raised in running. When he saw Theseus with the sword in his hand coming to meet him, he paused, for no one had ever faced him in that way before. Then he put his head down, and rushed forward, bellowing. But Theseus leaped quickly aside, and made a sharp thrust with his sword as he passed, and hewed off one of the monster's legs above the knee.

The Minotaur fell upon the ground, roaring and groaning and beating wildly about with his horned head and his hoof-like fists; but Theseus nimbly ran up to him and thrust the sword into his heart, and was away again before the beast could harm him. A great stream of blood gushed from the wound, and soon the Minotaur turned his face towards the sky and was dead.

Then the youths and maidens ran to Theseus and kissed his hands and feet, and thanked him for his great deed; and, as it was already growing dark, Theseus bade them follow him while he wound up the silken thread which was to lead them out of the Labyrinth. Through a thousand rooms and courts and winding ways they went, and at midnight they came to the outer door and saw the city lying in the moonlight before them; and, only a little way off, was the seashore where the black ship was moored which had brought them to Crete. The door was wide open, and beside it stood Ariadne waiting for them.

"The wind is fair, the sea is smooth, and the sailors are ready," she whispered; and she took the arm of Theseus, and all went together through the silent streets to the ship.

When the morning dawned they were far out to sea, and, looking back from the deck of the little vessel, only the white tops of the Cretan mountains were in sight.

Minos, when he arose from sleep, did not know that the youths and maidens had gotten safe out of the Labyrinth. But when Ariadne could not be found, he thought that robbers had carried her away. He sent soldiers out to search for her among the hills and mountains, never dreaming that she was now well on the way towards distant Athens.

Many days passed, and at last the searchers returned and said that the princess could nowhere be found. Then the king covered his head and wept, and said:

"Now, indeed, I am bereft of all my treasures!"

In the meanwhile, King AEgeus of Athens had sat day after day on a rock by the shore, looking and watching if by chance he might see a ship coming from the south. At last the vessel with Theseus and his companions hove in sight, but it still carried only the black sail, for in their joy the young men had forgotten to raise the white one.

"Alas! Alas! My son has perished!" moaned AEgeus; and he fainted and fell forward into the sea and was drowned. And that sea, from then until now, has been called by his name, the Aegean Sea.

Thus Theseus became king of Athens.

Story copied from www.greekmythology.com

Chapter IV

SLAUGHTER OF INNOCENCE

There is no "I" in the "we".
-Sandi King

Two years after the marriage, Marc agreed to support my getting a degree, but not the Psychology or Architecture degree which I wanted.

He gave me three choices: Electronics, Computer Information Systems or Accounting. I chose the last. Five years later in 1999, I graduated from California State Hayward University.

It would seem I had it all and I ought to be "happy", yet my life seemed like a borrowed one.

Marriage had become more like an unspoken contractual agreement. I was responsible for taking care of all Marc's needs and eventually I become like an appendage to him. In exchange he would give me room and board. It was not a marriage borne out of love, but more out of need and gratitude for what I had been given.

He did not want children and I had decided that I would not force that upon him. It was important to me that my children were planned and not an accident, like I was.

Marc was constantly working and drinking a fifth of a bottle of Scotch regularly to cope with his stressful job. I focused on my role as his personal housekeeper-always ready to take care of any need or request he had. He became my focus. After all, that is what I had been taught—to take care of a man and serve him well so he would keep me.

Years passed and I gave up the idea of ever being a mother, even though it had been one of the greatest wishes I had in life since I was fifteen years old. To my surprise, after ten years of being together he told me he was ready to be a father and so like a "good girl" I went with what he decided. I had no voice of my own.

My pregnancies were horrendous to the point of having a TPN (Total Parental Nutrition) line going directly into my heart because I was unable to eat or drink anything. The nausea and vomiting were debilitating. I carried a backpack with a nurse coming to the house daily to change the line.

After two intense high-risk pregnancies (2002 & 2005), constantly taking care of the house, his needs and the children I was to the point of exhaustion and depletion. I told him I was no longer able to take care of him and needed to concentrate on the children's needs. He was upset and the void between us grew. In a way I had trained him to depend on me and now I was dropping him like a rock. It was obvious that he was hurt.

My body had given up and to ensure the children had their needs met, I had to make them my priority. It was physically impossible for me to do everything. I agreed to stay under the same roof so my children would at least have their father in close proximity.

One day, while standing by the opening of the living room it became clear to me that my sacrifice to continue to stay in the marriage was useless. I saw my girls playing and calling for their daddy's attention while three steps away he was engrossed in his laptop computer, television on, earphones, reaching for his Scotch and completely disregarding them. At that moment I realized I would be staying for nothing, and knew the marriage was over.

I felt the immensity of the task at hand - of escaping this cage – yet I was unable to comprehend how I could dare to make such a leap across to the other shore to my freedom, to my individuality.

It would require a miracle to accomplish the difficult and dangerous task of finding my self again.

My whole body was about to collapse and I was going berserk. How could I make such a jump simply on a leap of faith? The road ahead was pitch black, with little or no indication. How would I know if I was headed in the right direction? My whole system seemed against it all; it felt like the threat of death, of annihilation.

There was a deep desire to be free, to kill the beast that robbed me of my innocence, yet I felt the terror overwhelming me.

Even if I found the courage to enter the labyrinth and face the beast, would I be able to find my way out?

My whole mind was vehemently against it. How could I bring my body to the task of supporting me in order to enter the darkness and venture into the unknown?

The only way was to push through by sheer will. I would leverage the same will I had used to suppress my essence during childhood, to go against my self to fit into the group.

That is all I had. The will to survive against all odds in the world of physicality, would be used to bend the defense mechanism, the maximum-security prison of the mind keeping me prisoner.

The gate surrounding my self seemed like three revolving vault doors. Escaping would be like going into an ever-darker space, into an abyss.

And then? I had no clue how I would do it. All I could perceive was this huge wheel of time spinning a million miles per hour and I was being asked to stop it. I was going crazy.

Then I realized that I had constantly tried to control by overcompensating. I had lived in fear all my life and because of this, I have remained in the personal submission that had caused a tremendous internal fragmentation of my self - the real inner me.

Chapter V

FLICKERING FLAME

You must be ready to burn yourself in your own flame,
how could you rise anew if you have not first become ashes?
-Friedrich Nietzsche

How did I get here? Who am I? Why do I feel detached, so disconnected from it all? It was as if life had been sucked out of me.

I had a nice home in a beautiful neighborhood, yet I felt that everything was missing. I had two beautiful daughters, a husband providing for all our physical needs and yet, I was not happy. Wasn't Cinderella supposed to live happily ever after? I thought I had it all. What was missing?

I sensed a faint voice in the far distance, a voice beyond consciousness beckoning me. I could barely sense it. I felt numb and could barely make sense of things anymore. I walked in complete numbness.

How had this happened? Why did it get harder? Life almost seemed in reverse, the harder I tried, the harder it got. I had it all; I made it. Those around me told me so. And why did I feel my life was falling apart? Why was I falling apart? Why is it that my life was not working after all the efforts I had made? I had done everything the way I had been told to and yet, misery is all I felt.

Who am I?

My days were as monotonous as they could be and I found myself depleted and dissolute, my spark gone. Where was the Cinderella dream I was sold into that did not work? Where was my charming prince? Why was I not living happily ever after? I felt the light inside going out of me. I was dying.... inside.

What happened? I had supposedly done everything in the way that guaranteed success. I followed the guidance of others along my path. If I followed the rules I would be happy, I would find the gold at the end of the rainbow. I had done it all by the book but here I was barely feeling alive.

I had reached the end of the line, nothing was working; the palace had become a castle surrounded by thorns, the prince a scary beast. I won't take it anymore. I need to get out of here, out of this constraining house surrounded by darkness.

Nothing was adding up. If they were right, then how is it that my life is a wreck? Yes, it looks great on the outside but I feel and look miserable. Why is it that my life is not working, why after listening to everyone about how to live a life and then having attained all the glories, I find myself struggling in a bottomless pit?

Voiceless sounds continually beckon me. Everything around me is pitch black, without any signs of anything. Where should I start? Where am I going? Something is calling me to leave; staying would mean the death of my soul, of my being.

Was this a call to expose the decay in my life so I could improve it for the better? How could I do it when the fear was so debilitating? I have spent my life in pursuit of this dream that was now disintegrating.

So, here I was feeling completely lost and overwhelmed by fear. How could I handle starting from zero with two small daughters on my own? I had not worked outside the house during the thirteen years of marriage! I felt useless and devalued. It was crazy! I remembered my hard struggles as a younger woman, hardly able to make it on my own. How could I do it now at age forty and with two children who needed me constantly?

My soul, my being, is dying; and the soft voice in the distance continues to beckon me to leave the safety of the shore. I feel as if I am in a storm in the middle of the ocean; I can hardly hear the whisper. It is far and I am so weak that I can barely make sense of my surroundings.

Yet, there is a part of me that knows what I must do and almost miraculously I started to prepare for what I sensed would be a long journey.

Thus a journey of a thousand years began with one-step at a time and all uphill. I made the decision to divorce and moved out of the house with my three and five year old daughters.

It was almost as if I knew it was going to be ~~for~~ a long ride, because a week earlier I had ordered seven books to bring with me. It did not make sense! I had never been a reader; I couldn't even recall ever having finished reading a book in my life.

Yet, I listened to the soft voice that continued to beckon me. I knew I if I stayed I would die because I could feel the light fading within, extinguishing forever.

I found myself between contradictions, between listening to a whispering voice of my soul calling me to my true essence, but fearing the loss of personal freedom, or worse, of punishment.

Torn between feelings of wanting to stay apart, yet fearing threats of becoming lost and being wrong; I had forgotten my place within the breath of life itself. I felt unrecognized; just another number, an old rag, a puppet dumped in the attic and forgotten. Yet the breath of life within beckoned so strongly

The whispering voice of my soul continued to beckon me to recognize the duress it was under and to awaken to its magnificent legacy; one honored by the breath of life itself!

It was not clear to me at the time, but I was a long way from my true essence. Miraculously, my willingness to follow the dim whisper was to be stronger than my denial. It seemed as if I was at the brink of madness. The fear seemed overwhelming.

Later I would realize that only a fool would dare take on such a task, for the road was not an easy one to travel; killing the Minotaur roaming the labyrinth of the mind would require a strong will and a firm and focused commitment to stay on course.

What was the truth? Was it truth that I had been born a sinful beast unworthy of my own existence? Was it truth that I must live in misery for the rest of my life? Who was telling the truth?

A rude awakening became obvious when I stepped into the world on my own on December 2007, with two young children to take care of and no support system. I would hire babysitters and always some issue emerged that I had to deal with.

My little one who was three years at the time was super active and unruly to the point that no babysitter could handle her. And after two years of constantly stopping and starting and not being able to handle raising the children and keep a job, I finally surrendered to not being able to hold a job.

A child psychologist diagnosed that my children would not make it in the public school system due to their high intelligence level and recommended placing them in a Waldorf/Montessori school environment.

I informed the father of my decision to home school the children and though he was not supportive he deferred on the decision so that he would not have to deal with it.

In January 2011 I pulled them out of public school and within less than a month there was incredible progress in the children's personality and behavior. This was especially so with the youngest who was now 6 years old.

Finally, after years of struggling I felt confident that I was getting my family back on track. The girls were getting along and we were experiencing happy times. The home schooling was giving them a sense of safety and stability. I would deal with my career later down the road, once they were older.

In May 2011, everything came tumbling down.

It came about after following the advice of my attorney to go back to Family Court to fix a $125.00 "technical error" in the divorce settlement, which I did not think was worth the effort.

I trembled at the idea of confronting the father of my children once again. I feared his wrath, but my attorney insisted otherwise I would be faced with an IRS audit.

So I followed the attorney's advice and what came next altered my destiny and the destiny of my children in a horrendous and traumatic way.

At court in a surprise move, the girl's father presented a motion disagreeing with homeschooling the children. I had been unable to attend as my attorney felt it was not necessary.

My absence in court was viewed as an act of disrespect and the judge ruled in the father's favor; *ordering the children to go back to the public school they had been pulled out of in January.*

I learned the news over the phone in Colorado while I was taking an energy-reading seminar. What a blow beneath the belt! I felt utterly devastated and powerless.

Chapter VI

BREAKING POINT

In all of us, even in good beings, there is a lawless wild-beast nature, which peers out in sleep.
-Socrates

When I returned from Colorado I tried for two weeks to reach an agreement with Marc. I shared with him how well the girls were doing with the homeschooling program.

I tried to convince him to allow me to continue doing it and give up the fight. However he would not listen and so I had to accept defeat and prepare my girls for the inevitable return to the school they hated.

That led to my sitting handcuffed in a police car for two hours. What follows is my literal recollection as requested to my Attorney following the event:

"I registered the girls at the public school on Monday morning around 10:30 am, then went to the School District and submitted the Transfer Form. I was told *that the girls could start school the next day* (Tuesday). They *asked if the father was in agreement* and I told them *that he was not, that I was ordered by the Court to bring the girls back.*

I called the manager at the public school on Tuesday morning around 8:00 am (May 10) and *asked if all the paperwork had gone through.* She said *that they were waiting to hear from me.* I said *the girls were ready and could be there within 30 minutes.* I needed to talk to the girls once again and prepare them for this, so I took them for cocoa and a muffin after breakfast so they were having fun before I took them to school.

Around 9:30 am on the way there, Anne, my 8 year old started to cry saying she did not want to go. I said *she needed to go, that I knew how strong she was to handle the requirement. Also that I could go to jail if she did not go to school because I was the adult taking care of her.* I reminded her that *I was here for her and I knew how strong she was.* She continued to cry and she said she wanted to call her father. I have never denied that and handed her the phone to call him.

Anne told him *she did not want to go, as she had been very unhappy in that public school. Also she did not understand why she had to go so soon and not in three or four weeks*. The father said that she "*needed to go; that it was all your mother's fault because she is taking me to Court.*" She continued *to insist over and over not to go. Then she told him we were almost there but that she did not want to go.*

I parked my car in an effort to handle the situation. I thought about taking Rochelle (the 6 year old) in first. I went into the school office and *asked if I should bring them to the office, and was advised to first take them to the classrooms*. I proceed with Rochelle towards the Kindergarten classroom but was distracted with Anne yelling and crying in the car.

At that moment a friend called and asked how the girls were doing, I *replied that the older one was very distressed. She then suggested I record how difficult this was for her, so I could show that I was complying with the Court but she needed a little bit more time to ease them into returning back to that particular Public School.*

As I went towards the car the Principal came out of her office telling me: *"Really, children do have a say in this. They need to be brought in."* Then I asked her not to interfere and told her, *"This is my family, and I will handle the situation."*

The public school principal insisted and followed me to my car, where Anne refused to get out. I asked the Principal to stay away and respect the space. She insisted. Then I told her that she could have been taking care of things six months ago when my other girl, Rochelle, had behavioral issues and was mistreated by her teacher and punished and coerced to eat food she did not like before she could get out of the room for recess.

The Principal said that she would call the police; I told her I was calling the police too.

While all this was happening, my friend Carol was on the phone. After I asked the Principal to give us our space to work our things through, I spoke with Carol and she asked to let her talk to the father of my children.

I called and asked him to talk to her which he refused, and preceded to call me "crazy." Carol told me she was calling the police.

Then the police arrived. One police officer, at the Principal's request and the other one requested by Carol to support me. I explained the situation about complying with the Court order and that my daughter Anne (the 8 year old) was having difficulty complying with. They said *that it was not her choice and that I needed to "force her" to go to school.*

I told them that I did not “force” my children. That is not the way I treated them. It seemed obvious to me that she needed more time to get used to the drastic change which was about to start again in a place she was having hard time going back to. I also wondered how I could force her, given that she was 90 lbs. and I was 120 lbs.? Physically it was not possible.

Officer Sam told me *that if I did not force her, then he would do it. He asked me to leave him alone with Anne.* I stepped aside and I observed how he was talking to her and explaining to her that she needed to do it.

While he was talking to her from the side rear window, I walked toward the driver seat to get my phone to call my lawyer, and asked him what to do in this situation. Before I could open the door, Officer Sam *ordered me to "stop."* I told him "*I am getting my phone to call my lawyer*." He said, "*You do not get anything!*

Sit!"

It took me a second to wonder, sit where? I thought to myself: *"Where? Right in the middle of the street?"* He then proceeded to come towards me and both officers handcuffed me. They told *me that I was obstructing the law*. I asked them, "*by getting my phone?*"

I asked them to allow me to speak with my attorney and Officer Sam replied: *"You don't get anything.*" When I insisted, he replied, *"You don't have any rights."*

As Officer Sam put me in the back of the police car I asked him to call Peter Cornwell and he told me "*I know Peter Cornwell*" and walked away, leaving me handcuffed in the back seat of the police car.

I watched my girls crying louder and louder watching me being handcuffed and put in the police car.

Officer Sam came back about 15 minutes later *and told me to reconsider and force Anne to get into school.*

I told him that *I could not do it because that was against my principles*.

He told me: *"Sometimes principles needed to be put aside. How could you permit your daughters to watch their mother being handcuffed instead of forcing them to go to school?"*

I told him *that Jesus stood for what he believed* and Officer Sam said, "Well, *he was the only one that had done that.*"

I repeated to him *that I did not force my children, I talked to them, I reasoned with them*.

He *expressed his disgust* and walking away from the police car said, *"No wonder the world has the problems it has, because of parents like you."*

Then, I watched my girls being brought into the school by their father. The officers proceeded to make phone calls.

Then Officer Sam came back and said I *was going to be taken to jail and that I could probably be released by Friday.*

I asked *why I was being arrested.* He said *something about what "booked" and being "arrested" meant*; I did not quite understand the context.

Then he told me: *"The question is who do you want to take care of your daughters until you are released?"*

He said, *"I guess they will go with their father or what do you prefer?"* I asked him *if they could go to one of my friends.* He said, *"No, either they go with their father or they go to a foster home."*

I paused couple of moments and said, *"It is obvious the father does not care about the well-being of our girls... I prefer they go to a foster home."*

He looked at me surprised. I said, "*The father has not shown any regard for their emotional well-being. Maybe a stranger will care more.*"

Officer Sam left and I stayed handcuffed in the back of the car without air-conditioning. I observed the officers calling and looking at books, as if trying to figure out what to do.

Fifteen minutes later, another officer came by. It seemed he had more superiority. He asked the officer to roll the window down and leave the door unlocked.

He asked me through the window *if I knew the reason I was there.* I told him *"No."* He showed me the Court order *saying that the children needed to be "re-enrolled" in a local public school and that I was not complying.*

I told him *I was complying. I registered the children yesterday, I filled out the paper work, I packed their lunches, I was parked in front of the school. Yet, obviously my daughter was having difficulty with it and you were asking me to force her. How could I force her? I have talked to her, explained to her and she seemed fine until we got here. She just needs more time to get used to the idea. This has happened too fast for her.*

The Superior Officer left and *asked the officer to keep the AC running and to make sure I was comfortable*. I was sweating profusely after an hour and a half of being kept in the back of the car under the heat of the day with my hands handcuffed behind my back.

Finally at 12:00 pm they released me and gave me a yellow paper that said I was detained for 2 hours.

After I thanked him, I was heading toward the school to see my girls and tell them I was fine. Officer Sam told me that *he did not recommend it because the Principal had been ready to ask them to arrest me.* He told me *to come back and pick up my girls after school*. I followed his instructions and left.

I went back to the Public School around 1:00 pm and waited on the curve for the school period to end. While I was waiting, the father of my girls called and said that *he would like to pick up the girls at school and have them spend the night at his house*.

I asked him why. He said "*because they are pretty worked up and we need to talk*". I responded *that I did not agree to that, that I was the Custodial Parent, that I was responsible for the girls needs and that I believed that it was important for them to see me and know that everything was going to be okay, and that we were going to get through this. And that he could see them and call them anytime but that the girls were coming with me.*

He asked *if I was going to bring them to school tomorrow*. I said *that not tomorrow because they had a doctor's appointment.* He asked me *what time and with whom*. I answered, "*With Dr. P at the S Center until 12:00 pm", and that I would bring them to the Public School on Wednesday*.

Five minutes later he called "*I am informing you that I have spoken with the Principal and she wants the girls back tomorrow after they are done with their appointment.*" I responded: "*You are giving our parents' rights away, they are our children not theirs.*"

I told him *that he had caused enough damage already and that anything he had to tell me, he needed to contact my attorney*. I hung up.

I was talking with my attorney on the cell phone, when I saw the girl's father arriving at the school grounds. I wondered why he was there.

My attorney recommended me to go into the office and request to be included in whatever conversations they were having. I went in and asked them to see the father of my girls and they told me to sit and wait. I waited and waited.

Fifteen minutes later I asked why my girls were not being released to me. They told me that they were waiting for the police to come and decide that.

Another fifteen minutes passed and at 2:30 pm Officer Sam came and said that he had spoken with the attorney, and that according to the divorce documents the father and I shared custody, he had the right to take the girls with him, and that because of my attitude he was allowing the father to have custody.

He told me *that I needed to go to Court if I wanted to change that.* He asked me *to leave the premises immediately because he did not want any "scene."*

I left without saying a word, completely devastated with what had happened. Not even the worse parents received this treatment. I, who have devoted my entire life for my girls, was being treated like the worst mother.

My head was spinning with unanswered questions: How is it that I did not have rights? How is it that my children had been ripped away from me just like that? How was I to protect them from emotional distress? Why were technicalities more important than their mental health? Was this really happening?

... ________ ...

Something snapped within me that morning. I refused to comply with an authority asking me to go against my values. I had just promised my children a week earlier that I would not disrespect them ever again, I had just promised to honor them and break the tradition of autocracy of my ancestors, that I would not force them to do anything.

That morning, while sitting in that police car, handcuffed and hyperventilating, images came of the Christ stripped of his clothes, mocked by Roman soldiers and a crown of thorns shoved on his head and a voice kept repeating and repeating: "Tear down the structure, tear down the structure."

Nothing made sense. I simply froze and refused to comply with their demands even though I was told my children would be going to a foster home if I did not force my child out of the car and into the school. During the time I had spent in the back of that police car, I continued to receive intense images of that event with the Christ.

I almost passed out as officers went back and forth referring to books and manuals. Two hours later they released me telling me to come back at the end of school to fetch my children.

I did come back and was told by the police that given my attitude they were giving my children to their father and that if I wished to get them back, I needed to go to Family Court. I was in complete shock and speechless as I walked away from the school. My attorney was also in disbelief.

My life had turned 180 degrees within hours and it would take two years and all my resources to get my children back. In time I would realize that even though it was excruciatingly painful, this event would be a turning point for the better.

How was I to accomplish such a dare, only with determination? It seemed pure madness. Yet, my earlier training in heavy physical work from the age of seven was now useful. I seemed to have a will of steel, how else could I survive the constant brutality of my caregivers and everyone I have encountered in my life? Here was an opportunity to break the walls encasing my soul. The same will I had used to suppress my needs, my desires, and my dreams would now have to sustain me on the journey out of the crazy labyrinth I found myself in.

Chapter VII

LABYRINTH'S THRESHOLD

Sometimes, the only way to discover the truth is by entering the dark forest at night.
-Alessandra Marion Jouberteix

From one point of view, the situation was horrendous. The odds were stacked against me ever getting my girls back. Two police reports and one from the School Principal said that I had gone berserk and was a threat to my children. Even though they were made up, it was my word against the established authority, and they made a strong and solid case against me.

The children's father leveraged this police support for his financial advantage and to force placement of the girls back in a public school.

And as he was present (and I was not) he had obtained an emergency motion that I was emotionally and psychologically unstable. As a result I could only see my children for short periods of time through outrageously expensive supervised visitation. I was considered a "threat" to my children after being their 24-7 caregiver.

The court battle was stacked against me from all angles; the father was a blue-collar, college graduated, corporate law-abiding American citizen while I was a single mother, without a job, foreigner, who had "disrespected authority".

Not even my friends believed me when I told them that police reports were not telling the truth. In their opinion it was useless to battle against a mighty court system. They thought that instead I should leave the country, redo my life and forget about my daughters.

It seemed impossible I could ever get my girls back, yet I was not going to give my daughters up. Somehow and some way, I had to do it. How, I had no idea.

Through my daring act to "disobey the police orders" (as earlier described), I had stepped out of their box. I had stood up and said *NO to authority when I had previously said yes all my life. Why was I now surprised?*

From the perspective of a male-dominated world it was true that "my attitude" was one of defiance. A simple "NO" had caused a tremendous shocking and rippling effect in our lives.

An effect that would prove to be an opportunity because living without my daughters gave me the space to be alone with the parts of me buried deeply within my psyche.

I went from being a full-time mother to now being by myself with no one to take care of. This allowed me to tune into my own inner self and find answers to what was happening and to delve into the deep dark corners within my psyche.

With attentive focus I set forth to engage in a personal journey which would include a detoxification period to clear and delete the old programs implanted in my brain while growing up, creating a new opportunity to meet my true self, my inner essence.

FIRE & HOPE

Gifts of Disobedience & Curiosity

In those old, old times, there lived two brothers who were not like other men, nor yet like those Mighty Ones who lived upon the mountaintop. They were the sons of one of those Titans who had fought against Zeus and been sent in chains to the strong prison-house of the Lower World.

The name of the elder of these brothers was Prometheus, or Forethought; for he was always thinking of the future and making things ready for what might happen to-morrow, or next week, or next year, or it may be in a hundred years to come. The younger was called Epimetheus, or Afterthought; for he was always so busy thinking of yesterday, or last year, or a hundred years ago, that he had no care at all for what might come to pass after a while.

For some cause Zeus had not sent these brothers to prison with the rest of the Titans.

Prometheus did not care to live amid the clouds on the mountaintop. He was too busy for that. While the Mighty Folk were spending their time in idleness, drinking nectar and eating ambrosia, he was intent upon plans for making the world wiser and better than it had ever been before.

He went out amongst men to live with them and help them; for his heart was filled with sadness when he found that they were no longer happy as they had been during the golden days when Saturn was king. Ah, how very poor and wretched they were! He found them living in caves and in holes of the earth, shivering with the cold because there was no fire, dying of starvation, hunted by wild beasts and by one another–the most miserable of all living creatures.

"If they only had fire," said Prometheus to himself, "they could at least warm themselves and cook their food; and after a while they could learn to make tools and build themselves houses. Without fire, they are worse off than the beasts."

Then he went boldly to Zeus and begged him to give fire to men, that so they might have a little comfort through the long, dreary months of winter.

"Not a spark will I give," said Zeus. "No, indeed! Why, if men had fire they might become strong and wise like ourselves, and after a while they would drive us out of our kingdom. Let them shiver with cold, and let them live like the beasts. It is best for them to be poor and ignorant, that so we Mighty Ones may thrive and be happy."

Prometheus made no answer; but he had set his heart on helping mankind, and he did not give up. He turned away, and left Zeus and his mighty company forever.

As he was walking by the shore of the sea he found a reed, or, as some say, a tall stalk of fennel, growing; and when he had broken it off he saw that its hollow center was filled with a dry, soft pith which would burn slowly and keep on fire a long time. He took the long stalk in his hands, and started with it towards the dwelling of the sun in the Far East.

"Mankind shall have fire in spite of the tyrant who sits on the mountain top," he said.

He reached the place of the sun in the early morning just as the glowing, golden orb was rising from the earth and beginning his daily journey through the sky. He touched the end of the long reed to the flames, and the dry pith caught on fire and burned slowly. Then he turned and hastened back to his own land, carrying with him the precious spark hidden in the hollow center of the plant.

He called some of the shivering men from their caves and built a fire for them, and showed them how to warm themselves by it and how to build other fires from the coals. Soon there was a cheerful blaze in every rude home in the land, and men and women gathered round it and were warm and happy, and thankful to Prometheus for the wonderful gift, which he had brought to them from the sun.

It was not long until they learned to cook their food and so to eat like men instead of like beasts. They began at once to leave off their wild and savage habits; and instead of lurking in the dark places of the world, they came out into the open air and the bright sunlight, and were glad because life had been given to them.

After that, Prometheus taught them, little by little, a thousand things. He showed them how to build houses of wood and stone, and how to tame sheep and cattle and make them useful, and how to plow and sow and reap, and how to protect themselves from the storms of winter and the beasts of the woods. Then he showed them how to dig in the earth for copper and iron, and how to melt the ore, and how to hammer it into shape and fashion from it the tools and weapons that they needed in peace and war; and when he saw how happy the world was becoming he cried out:

"A new Golden Age shall come, brighter and better by far than the old!"

Things might have gone on very happily indeed, and the Golden Age might really have come again, had it not been for Zeus. But one day, when he chanced to look down upon the earth, he saw the fires burning, and the people living in houses, and the flocks feeding on the hills, and the grain ripening in the fields, and this made him very angry.

"Who has done all this?" he asked.

And some one answered, "Prometheus!"

"What! That young Titan!" he cried. "Well, I will punish him in a way that will make him wish I had shut him up in the prison-house with his kinsfolk. But as for those puny men, let them keep their fire. I will make them ten times more miserable than they were before they had it."

Of course it would be easy enough to deal with Prometheus at any time, and so Zeus was in no great haste about it. He made up his mind to distress mankind first; and he thought of a plan for doing it in a very strange, roundabout way.

In the first place, he ordered his blacksmith Hephaestus, whose forge was in the crater of a burning mountain, to take a lump of clay which he gave him, and mold it into the form of a woman. Hephaestus did as he was bidden; and when he had finished the image, he carried it up to Zeus, who was sitting among the clouds with all the Mighty Folk around him. It was nothing but a mere lifeless body, but the great blacksmith had given it a form more perfect than that of any statue that has ever been made.

"Come now!" said Zeus, "let us all give some goodly gift to this woman;" and he began by giving her life.

Then the others came in their turn, each with a gift for the marvelous creature. One gave her beauty; and another a pleasant voice; and another good manners; and another a kind heart; and another skill in many arts; and, lastly, someone gave her curiosity. Then they called her Pandora, which means the all-gifted, because she had received gifts from them all.

Pandora was so beautiful and so wondrously gifted that no one could help loving her. When the Mighty Folk had admired her for a time, they gave her to Mercury, the light-footed; and he led her down the mountainside to the place where Prometheus and his brother were living and toiling for the good of mankind. He met Epimetheus first, and said to him:

"Epimetheus, here is a beautiful woman, whom Zeus has sent to you to be your wife."

Prometheus had often warned his brother to beware of any gift that Zeus might send, for he knew that the mighty tyrant could not be trusted; but when Epimetheus saw Pandora, how lovely and wise she was, he forgot all warnings, and took her home to live with him and be his wife.

Pandora was very happy in her new home; and even Prometheus, when he saw her, was pleased with her loveliness. She had brought with her a golden casket, which Zeus had given her at parting, and which he had told her held many precious things; but wise Athena, the queen of the air, had warned her never, never to open it, nor look at the things inside.

"They must be jewels," she said to herself; and then she thought of how they would add to her beauty if only she could wear them. "Why did Zeus give them to me if I should never use them, nor so much as look at them?" she asked.

The more she thought about the golden casket, the more curious she was to see what was in it; and every day she took it down from its shelf and felt of the lid, and tried to peer inside of it without opening it.

"Why should I care for what Athena told me?" she said at last. "She is not beautiful, and jewels would be of no use to her. I think that I will look at them, at any rate. Athena will never know. Nobody else will ever know."

She opened the lid a very little, just to peep inside. All at once there was a whirring, rustling sound, and before she could shut it down again, out flew ten thousand strange creatures with death-like faces and gaunt and dreadful forms, such as nobody in all the world had ever seen. They fluttered for a little while about the room, and then flew away to find dwelling-places wherever there were homes of men. They were diseases and cares; for up to that time mankind had not had any kind of sickness, nor felt any troubles of mind, nor worried about what the morrow might bring forth.

These creatures flew into every house, and, without any one seeing them, nestled down in the bosoms of men and women and children, and put an end to all their joy; and ever since that day they have been flitting and creeping, unseen and unheard, over all the land, bringing pain and sorrow and death into every household.

If Pandora had not shut down the lid so quickly, things would have gone much worse. But she closed it just in time to keep the last of the evil creatures from getting out. The name of this creature was Foreboding, and although he was almost half out of the casket, Pandora pushed him back and shut the lid so tight that he could never escape. If he had gone out into the world, men would have known from childhood just what troubles were going to come to them every day of their lives, and they would never have had any joy or hope so long as they lived.

And this was the way in which Zeus sought to make mankind more miserable than they had been before Prometheus had befriended them.

The next thing that Zeus did was to punish Prometheus for stealing fire from the sun. He bade two of his servants, whose names were Strength and Force, to seize the bold Titan and carry him to the topmost peak of the Caucasus Mountains. Then he sent the blacksmith Hephaestus to bind him with iron chains and fetter him to the rocks so that he could not move hand or foot.

Hephaestus did not like to do this, for he was a friend of Prometheus, and yet he did not dare to disobey. And so the great friend of men, who had given them fire and lifted them out of their wretchedness and shown them how to live, was chained to the mountain peak; and there he hung, with the storm-winds whistling always around him, and the pitiless hail beating in his face, and fierce eagles shrieking in his ears and tearing his body with their cruel claws. Yet he bore all his sufferings without a groan, and never would he beg for mercy or say that he was sorry for what he had done.

Year after year, and age after age, Prometheus hung there. Now and then old Helios, the driver of the sun car, would look down upon him and smile; now and then flocks of birds would bring him messages from far-off lands; once the ocean nymphs came and sang wonderful songs in his hearing; and oftentimes men looked up to him with pitying eyes, and cried out against the tyrant who had placed him there.

Then, once upon a time, a white cow passed that way,—a strangely beautiful cow, with large sad eyes and a face that seemed almost human. She stopped and looked up at the cold gray peak and the giant body which was chained there. Prometheus saw her and spoke to her kindly:

"I know who you are," he said. "You are Io who was once a fair and happy maiden in distant Argos; and now, because of the tyrant Zeus and his jealous queen, you are doomed to wander from land to land in that un human form. But do not lose hope. Go on to the southward and then to the west; and after many days you shall come to the great river Nile. There you shall again become a maiden, but fairer and more beautiful than before; and you shall become the wife of the king of that land, and shall give birth to a son, from whom shall spring the hero who will break my chains and set me free. As for me, I bide in patience the day which not even Zeus can hasten or delay. Farewell!"

Poor Io would have spoken, but she could not. Her sorrowful eyes looked once more at the suffering hero on the peak, and then she turned and began her long and tiresome journey to the land of the Nile.

Ages passed, and at last a great hero whose name was Hercules came to the land of the Caucasus. In spite of Zeus's dread thunderbolts and fearful storms of snow and sleet, he climbed the rugged mountain peak; he slew the fierce eagles that had so long tormented the helpless prisoner on those craggy heights; and with a mighty blow, he broke the fetters of Prometheus and set the grand old hero free.

"I knew that you would come," said Prometheus. "Ten generations ago I spoke of you to Io, who was afterwards the queen of the land of the Nile."

"And Io," said Hercules, "was the mother of the race from which I am sprung."

Story copied from www.greekmythology.com

Chapter VIII

FROZEN HEART

Oh, shatter the walls that encase my soul!
-Alessandra Marion Jouberteix

I had depended on strangers since my birth and my innate being had to stay backstage to ensure my physical survival. I had learned to adapt well, oh very well indeed. I learned the camouflage game very early and mastered it.

In order to survive, I learned to defer to others who supposedly knew better, with promises of happily ever after that had never come. I learned to follow the drum of others instead of my own and now here I was, at the blink of collapse.

Would it be possible to go from complete dependency to the other side of independence? Freedom? What freedom? I had no idea what it looked like, so how could I even be free? There was no image of freedom in my system, yet the world around me was now demanding that I go on with my life.

Are you dumb? Why don't you get it? Don't you see? You have to get a job, just like everybody else. Don't you see how the world works? Are you stupid or something? And so my self-talk ranted and raved continuously, incessantly.

There is a constant pulling in two directions, like a chariot with two horses pulling in opposite directions:

(1) Inside calling for life and

(2) Outside to serve the long-established physical structure.

I continued to feel this deep numbness, and the judgmental voices continuously torturing me.

Constantly repressing my emotions and watching them come out of me unbridled toward the beings that I loved most in this world, my own children. How could I be so harsh with them and so sweet at the same time?

Where did all these impulsive emotions originate? I considered myself a kind person, I have a good heart, I want to help the world, why did I continue going backwards instead of forward?

I understand mentally that as a child I was at the mercy of others for my survival. I know that choice was non-existent and did not develop the ability to make decisions; I conformed to the world around me. But I am an adult now, why is it that I can't function?

My heart had been wounded so deeply through life that I had shielded and barricaded it. I was not going to have my heart hurt again. Having survived the unthinkable had toughened me up. I felt so full of "crap" implanted from others that I was unable to see who or what the heck I was.

I felt as if I have been buried under massive concrete chunks. I felt immense frustration at not being able to liberate myself.

My mind was speeding at a million miles per hour and my limbs felt weak. My brain seemed to be in overload, full of junk programs, debilitating me.

How was I to stop the wheel of time racing uncontrollably? It felt as if I was being asked to open a vault with three feet thick walls and a triple security system. It was not just one door I had to open, but multiple ones. Opening one door only meant stepping into another one to figure out yet another layer. The amount of effort seemed insurmountable.

I found myself feeling completely lost and defeated. Without having a sense of life, how was I to find the strength to continue now that I found myself completely exhausted? It was as if my mind had taken control of life and I was just a puppet.

In a complete lost state, I felt completely and utterly unable to function, reaching and reaching for ways to function in a world that was collapsing around me.

Deep within me I perceive the overwhelming challenge I am facing, yet I am paralyzed. How does a heart freeze? How can I feel, when everything within me suppresses me, represses me, denies me?

The denial of my essence had blocked my self-expression, freezing my heart and only an act of true, unconditional love, could thaw it out.

Then, in the distance, a faint whisper murmurs *"it is hard, yet it is possible*".

Chapter IX

IN THE BEGINNING

Every living thing, every leaf, every bird, is only alive
because it contains the secret word for life.
That is the only difference between us, and a lump of clay.
A word. Words are life.
-The Book Thief

Mythology - traditional story about gods and heroes - parallels with philosophy, the study of the soul. It is through images that we convey messages to uplift or redirect our lives.

How else can we explain the massive explosion of media in our lives? Even the poorest person owns a television and a phone. Yet the challenge is not the stories we make, but that we believe them and even worse, get lost in them.

Indeed, our physical body is the apex of technology. Our five senses, the collectors of infinite experiences and our brain, the super archive retrieving and sorting the collected data, give us the optimum edge in the world we live in.

Our brain, the best super computer there is, knows exactly how to navigate the world, at least the world of the social group. It is a matter of survival that we learn what works and what does not, what is acceptable and what will get us in trouble.

We think that we have perfected our environment and have become super machines, ourselves. By the age of seven, children have established in their brain how a world structure works; the roadmap in how to function within the group.

Words are powerful and they convey deep meaning. Our intelligence is remarkable, yet we continue to disregard that brains may form abstract images; and the minute we speak a word without realizing it, an image is retracted from an internal filing system.

Do you ever wonder why it is that when we say we will not perform a certain task, we find ourselves doing just exactly that? Why is it that our thoughts are different from our actions? Why is it that we continue to talk about saving the world and yet the world appears to get worse? Why are we so full of contradictions?

A story told by generations shaped my reality without me even realizing. Because of this story told by my caregivers and which I believed to be true, I was called into a journey of self-discovery to uncover the true essence of my being, which was buried long, long ago...

It is my hope that you begin remembering the core of your being and realize that your life may probably be running according to an automatic pilot system installed there long ago to ensure your survival, just like mine.

Here is that story:

"Once upon a time, out of void and nothingness God created the heavens and the earth. Then he formed a man, Adam, from the dust of the ground and breathed into his nostrils the breath of life, and the man became a living being.

God then placed Adam in the Garden of Eden where all kinds of trees grow out of the ground—trees that were pleasing to the eye and good for food. In the middle of the garden there were two trees; The Tree of Life and The Tree of Knowledge of Good and Evil.

God commanded: "you are free to eat from any tree in the garden; but you must not eat from The Tree of Knowledge of Good and Evil, for when you eat from it you will certainly die.' Then God said, 'It is not good for man to be alone.'

So, God caused the man to fall into a deep sleep; and while he was sleeping, he took one of his ribs and made a woman with it, and he brought her to the man. The man said, 'This is now a bone of my bones and flesh of my flesh; she shall be called 'woman,' for she was taken out of man.'

One morning, the serpent that was craftier than any of the wild animals that God had made, said to the woman, "God knows that when you eat the fruit from the Tree of Knowledge of Good and Evil your eyes will be opened, and you will be like God.

Eve took some and ate it and also gave some to her husband. Then the eyes of both of them were opened, and they realized they were naked; so they sewed fig leaves together and made coverings for themselves...

Later in the afternoon, when God called them, they hid among the trees of the garden. But God called again. Adam answered, 'I heard you in the garden, and I was afraid because I was naked; so I hid.'

And he said, 'who told you that you were naked? Have you eaten from the tree that I commanded you not to eat from? "The man said, 'The woman you put here with me—she gave me some fruit from the tree, and I ate it.'

Then the Lord God said to the woman, 'What is this you have done?' The woman said, 'the serpent deceived me, and I ate. So the Lord God said to the serpent, 'because you have done this, cursed are you above all livestock and all wild animals! You will crawl on your belly and you will eat dust all the days of your life. And I will put enmity between you and the woman, and between your offspring and hers he will crush your head and you will strike his heel.'

To the woman he said," I will make your pains in child bearing very severe; with painful labor you will give birth to children. Your desire will be for your husband, and he will rule over you.'

To Adam he said, 'because you listened to your wife and ate fruit from the tree about which I commanded you, 'You must not eat from it,' "Cursed is the ground because of you, through painful toil you will eat food from in all the days of your life. It will produce thorns and thistles for you, and you will eat the plants of the field. By the sweat of your brow, you will eat your food until you return to the ground, since from it you were taken, for dust you are and to dust you will return.'

So the Lord God banished him from the Garden of Eden to work the ground from which he had been taken. After he drove the man out, he placed on the east side of the Garden of Eden cherubim and a flaming sword flashing back and forth to guard the way to the tree of life."

There is an innate tendency within to jump to conclusions and to make assumptions. Our brain cannot comprehend infinity, life force. It is the brain's tendency to box things in; it is only through compartmentalization that it is able to make sense.

God as life force, pure expression cannot be perceived by the five senses. Is God really that petty to give a damn about our petty quarrels? Our gullibility is our greatest weakness; we do not stay alert and fall into relying on others to take care of things for us, to tell us how it is without questioning.

I often wonder why the story in the Bible referred to an Apple. In the culture proceeding Christianity, the apple was the fruit of the gods. Aphrodite was depicted with an apple. Was this a clear display to discredit the Goddess of Love and Sensuality? Was this done on purpose to establish the new set of rules of their so-called "morality"?

Does it become clear to perceive that when Christianity replaced Greek culture, it made complete sense to create new interpretation of stories to destroy the symbols represented by the old culture?

Is this not what is commonly done to rally the masses against the old to embrace the new? History is filled with facts and yet, why do we continue to believe what is staring us in the face?

A clear example of the old culture embedded in the new is the depiction of the Christian God that looks like Zeus, the Greek God.

My mind would retrieve the image of the Sistine Chapel ceiling by Michelangelo every time I would think of God. Yet, we are not supposed to create an image of God.

Also, wasn't the serpent connected to Mother Goddess in many previous cultures?

At the Oracle of Delphi, a snake would whisper prophecies to the priestess, a woman. Does it not make complete sense to choose the snake and vilify it?

Women had a strong social and political position before Christianity took over, and this story simply cements the new order, the patriarchy.

Women lost their position of priestesses, when Christianity took over. Was the shame and blame game a plot to vilify women and bring them into compliance? Was this story simply a tool to legitimize men as the only ones able to hold power? How can a single story bring so many contradictions?

The new order used the power of imagination well to instill fear in an already dark world. It only takes 40 days to establish a new habit in the system.

Have you ever thought what 2000 years of shame, guilt and blame have done to our psyche? And we wonder why we experience continual suffering and are a living contradiction?

Have we underestimated the power of imagination?

Chapter X

RUPTURE

What tears us down will eventually open us to life
-Alessandra Marion Jouberteix

Humans are natural storytellers. Heavily influenced by Christian stories while growing up, the story of the expulsion of Adam and Eve from the Garden of Eden carried a heavy imprint in my psyche. Because I was told I was born sinful, I would spend all my life trying to wash off the sinfulness within me so I could get back into the Garden.

Being told I was born unworthy set the tone. The story of Adam and Eve established and maintained a reality of male dominance in my life and the belief that a woman was nothing without a man or his recognition. This seemingly harmless story masterfully influenced my behavior.

Eve's act of defiance to disobey God and therefore his representative on Earth which happened to be men, was the promise of doom and eternal punishment that I dreaded.

This, I was told, was the story of human kind and if I thought that I could get pleasure and wisdom from doing forbidden things, I would get neither.

My life would be ruined if I "sinned" or disobeyed. Doing wrong would get me into trouble and bring other bad results.

My inner intuitive understanding, connected to a consciousness receptive to a direct revelation of truth, would be considered unnatural and sacrilegious.

My insistence on this intuition would send a clear message of disobedience to the established male ruling God. I was expected to obey those in authority, to submit in all things if I was to survive, and so I did.

Most stories as I recall are to inspire us and to uplift us. We see that "bad" guys usually do not win because in the end, the "good" guys win. There is a moral to the story which is always for the better. Yet, the story of the Garden is quite unique in that regard; someone took a mishap and the descendants were to suffer misery for eons to come.

This story in the Bible designed to influence and alter my view of reality, denied my inalienable rights and placed me in an "object" position. There was no way out of the legacy of shame by my ancestors. I was to have a life of pain and suffering without end.

The relentless indoctrination caused a deep fragmentation in my psyche and continued to tear me apart well into my adulthood. The fear of punishment would engulf all aspects of my life, creating a slave mentality within me.

I have been told that winners write history. The common practice is to re-write all the books and refashion all ideas so as to make them fit the requirements of the men in power.

The written word of the first half of our Bible, which has profoundly affected our Western minds, took place about hundred years after Aeschylus wrote the Greek Tragedy called Oresteia, where mother-murder was no crime.

There is overwhelming evidence supporting all the horrific acts performed in the name of "God." Plenty of facts abound in our history books of those abusing their power to force the ruled, into compliance. Even in today's world, a quick look reflects how easily persuaded we are by the strategies of the media. We are easily swayed into believing what we are told without questioning it. Knowing this at an intellectual level is simple and yet we are full of contradictions. We say one thing and do another, addictions are rampant, and depression abounds. Even though facts are plentiful, we remain deeply dissatisfied with our lives.

As children our imagination is fully open and because our trust rests fully in our caregivers, their words and actions imprint an indelible image deep within our psyche.

Because of our openness to be easily persuaded, stories convey an abstract message in form of an image, and just like software programs, these images continue to play in the background without our noticing them.

Stories are so real to us, just like the monster under the bed, and our desire to belong is stronger, creating a deep vulnerability at the core of our being; our survival depends heavily on our caregivers, the group.

My realization of the heavy imprint of this story within me, gives me the impulse to share the terrible damage I believe it has created in all of us, especially women.

So much human error and dysfunction from our ancestors have continued to pass down from generation to generation and I believe it is stored in the total human memory and in the memory of a family line, just like it would be in the Mainframe of a computer. There is no way to avoid our collective inheritance, but there is a way to transmute it.

True morality seeks for the betterment of all, and therefore this story is immoral when it only delivers a message of shamefulness surrounding our humanness. A heavy burden has been carried within our soul setting the stage of guilt and blame, and creating a soil where only punishment and self-flagellation exists. What goodness can sprout from a beginning of shame? All of us, men and women, lost our integrity since birth under such demeaning conditions. A shameful birth in a hopeless place is simply a defeat from the start.

Because I believed at the core of my being that I was the product of the most shameful beings ever existed, I felt powerless and enslaved in my own skin.

Chapter XI

MENDING THE WOUND

The limits of my language are the limits of my world
-Ludwig Wittgenstein

Inscription above the entrance to the Temple of Apollo at Delphi reads: "Know thyself."

How can we really know ourselves when what the world reflects back is only contradiction? I have gotten lost in definitions and concepts, should and should not's, right and wrong; I felt I was in total overload, unrecognizable, unable to figure out what to do.

I had depended on others to tell me what to do, how to do it, I had followed well, and now I was on my own at the age of forty and on top of everything, with two daughters to fend for. How was I going to survive? I had always been at the expense of the goodwill of others.

I wished to be just like everyone else, to belong, to be pretty, and to be part of the group. I traded my essence, my unique expression in exchange for safety and protection.

My observation of the mechanics of the physical world demonstrated the dynamics of operation; this is how things work, only to find out now that they did not. I did not know who I was, covered with all the conditioning and programming imposed by the group.

Deep in the labyrinth, when looking at the feared beast I realized that it was simply the denial of me and the misalignment experienced as disharmony and unhappiness.

The Minotaur was my own split personality, pulling in both directions at once struggling to be free from fears and attachments, just like pressing the gas and brake pedals.

Facing the Minotaur meant facing my own projections and the stories I had created along the way based on my assumptions, were eye openers. Just like telling a child there is no monster under the bed does not get rid of the monster in the child's head. We must go looking for the beast under the bed and face it.

It seemed that my brain had stored all the experiences and that now these files were being retrieved trying to find a solution to the situations I was facing and nothing would work. And here I was, facing the projections and watching them disappear in front of my eyes, like magic.

Had I created it all? Was it all a story? I wanted to kill the Minotaur, my wild spirit, when all it was asking me to do was to reconcile it by simply accepting it and quit rejecting it.

What was causing my suffering was my insistence on being only a "civilized" creature. As a child I believed the story that there was nothing good within me and that I had to purge myself from my ancestors' disobedience, and bury my own hidden power and stamina.

As a child I was highly persuaded by my caregivers and considered them highly organized beings that understood the order of things and the balance of harmony and discipline.

Yet, I had gotten stuck on the story I heard and believed my own projections. I took upon myself to "break" my spirit so I could be civilized and belong.

Because I had willed myself to comply; I locked myself away and swallowed the key. I was scared of the wild part within me, the born free and unconditioned self.

My life had been full of contradictions; resisting the beast within me. But wait, who was the beast? Was this a reflection of how deeply I was attacking my self?

My caregivers thought me well and I had been a great learner after all, adapting fully. I saw judgment because religion thought me to be a good girl, to deny myself, the only way to expression was the internalization of judgment toward myself.

A reverse mirror! The beast was I! By judging myself I would find myself in the extremes of overcompensating. This act was never solution-oriented.

In Luke 14:26 Jesus speaks: "If anyone comes to me and does not hate father and mother, wife and children, brothers and sisters--yes even their own life--such a person cannot be my disciple."

Was he talking about breaking tradition? Leaving the story behind? Did I represent the essence of being? It had become clear that I was not and had not been my original self and it became necessary to walk away from all the stories that had programmed me and conditioned me.

What? This is what I had always desired all my life. To belong, to have the family I never had. I had been selling myself, trading my essence for safety, my survival.

My freedom called for bravery, strength and for courage to see the truth. The beast in front of me was me split in half; I wanted my freedom and my safety at the same time and that freedom could not be in the group because there was no "I" in the group, it is all about "we."

My suffering was simply my refusal to move out of my dilemma. I wanted it both ways; I wanted to be free and yet I allowed fear to be the driving force that was guiding me.

For my caregivers safety was the only concern and added to the power of words, their meaning and misinterpretation would prove poisonous—Images were splitting my psyche by being told I must love those beings who had shown only hate towards me.

My own self-imposed slavery, supported by fear, worry, and victimhood kept me boxed in. I thought I was not big enough or powerful enough to stand up.

My spirit was broken, and my inner flame extinguished.

As a child I grew up thinking that going against my caregivers, to disagree was dangerous. As a child, it is difficult to realize that it was far more dangerous to forfeit my right to speak up, to say no. Suffering became the norm and I adapted well to it.

As an adult, I continued the same pattern and allowed the man I married to assume my right of personal choice. Declining to make my own decisions accounted for the uncertainty and confusion surrounding my life.

Following the absent father's 2011 court battle to force the children back into public school, there were numerous court hearings one after another.

The strategy was to attack every angle at once; requesting full custody of the girls, cutting alimony and child support. Just like a war strategy to cut all supplies from the enemy line to force complete surrender.

The father submitted an emergency motion petitioning full custody claiming I was emotionally and psychologically unstable based solely on reports by the two policemen and School Principal described earlier. I continued showing up to court only to be sent back defeated each time.

However four months later, in September, I was "granted visitation" in a controlled environment with another person approved by the Court in mandatory attendance, at a cost of $400 for each 2-hour visit.

My children were experiencing tremendous heartache. My older daughter was so distraught that she **WANTED** to kill herself while the younger one was putting on a strong front and repressing it.

Friends urged me to give up the fight, saying there was so much evidence stacked up against me that it would be best to leave the country and rebuild my life. They urged me to forget about my girls, but how could I? I would fight until I could fight no more.

Then in December 2012, following an expensive, extensive and psychological evaluation of both parents, it was recommended that *the physical custody of the girls be given to the mother, and that the girls could attend a Waldorf Charter School.*

Yet, there was another hurdle to deal with. I spoke with my girls and told them I had done everything in my power. There was no more money to continue to fight. I embraced them and told them I had fought until the end. It was not up to me anymore.

In January 2013 the father's financial support was cut to zero. My assets from the divorce had been used up in the long process to get my girls back.

Without a penny in my pocket and a threat of eviction I sought Welfare help and received food stamps, while friends helped with rent money.

Three months later financial support from the father was reinstated, but severely cut to $1,800 a month based on the court's theoretical assumption that I could work 40 hours a week.

The girls attend a Waldorf Charter school that supports their creativity and are with their mother during the week. On weekends they drive 90 miles away to visit their father.

We have all been transformed by the experience, including the father. The girls love their school and are thriving. The battle was worth every ache and dollar spent for the children's well-being.

Choice gives us the opportunity to influence life's direction. It is easy to see why my soul was dying. I had given others my power. I had chosen to believe that others held the key of my life.

I had chosen to focus on blaming others and the circumstances for my experience. I had followed a life of conformity in which I gave up personal choice, not realizing that I was forfeiting my rights and giving up the opportunity to influence my life's direction. My own refusal to make decisions created the confusion in itself.

This freedom of choice was to be practiced and endured throughout the grueling Family court proceedings. It would take two years for my girls to get back home with me.

I would show up to court and would lose every argument, over and over again. My own friends would advise me to let it go, to keep my money and start a new life.

They would tell me that my girls would be fine, yet I knew they would not. I continued to plow along, burning through money like crazy, as if it was a bottomless pit.

My girls suffered and I suffered watching them suffer. I put my bootstraps and a happy face and continue the constant battle against the court system. My voice seemed to be mute, as if it did not matter. It was a nightmare.

I only knew I was not going to abandon my children like my mother had abandoned me. I would never forgive myself. I decided to do everything in my power to get them back even though it looked like a mission impossible.

I was under severe scrutiny; from being emotionally unstable to being lazy because I could not find a job. Everything was put on the stand against me and I faced it all.

I pulled all the money out of my 401K paying high taxes; declared bankruptcy, moved to Sacramento to try to become a Waldorf teacher, slept in my car, rented a room at a family's house to where I could have my children for the weekends.

I felt the whole world on my shoulders. I had given my power away a long time ago and to gain it back would mean to climb a very steep mountain. I had to stand up beating after beating until I could not go anymore.

Finally, after two years of severe pounding, the Custodial Evaluation came back recommending the girls come back to me. The father did not accept it and was ready to continue fighting me. I spoke with my girls and told them I had done everything and I had no more money to continue fighting for them.

That was it, without a penny in my reserves, it seemed my future would be on the street and without money I would be unable to see my girls. I surrender and showed up to court thinking it would be the last time.

The attorneys were able to persuade the father to let go, given that the custody report contained 50 pages, which meant we could be arguing in court for a long, long time. The father gave in and on January 7, 2013 my girls came home at last and were enrolled in a public charter school with Waldorf Curriculum. The fight had been endured and the triumphal joy was exquisite.

Chapter XII

CHOICE

Eve's Gift

Nature never breaks her own laws
-Leonardo Da Vinci

Have you ever wondered why in the story of the Garden it was an apple tempting Eve and not an orange? A fig? A grape? Wasn't the apple the symbol of Aphrodite in Greek mythology? And didn't the Greek culture precede Christianity? What historical figure solidified the Roman Empire when he converted to Christianity?

Could this story simply be a patchwork, an interpretation imposed under the new regime? Is it possible that the meaning got lost in translation? Was my belief based on the leaders of a mighty empire, a misinterpretation or a conscious decision to deceive?

When I looked into the way the brain works, I realized that my brain was constantly overcompensating... it was not interested in the wellbeing of the human endeavor, but only interested in predicting so it can control. And isn't through fear the best way to accomplish this?

The continual terror inflicted on the masses to force them into submission must have caused a tremendous internal fragmentation.

This made sense to me when I discovered an interesting fact: Monarch butterflies migrate from the South to Canada each year and the ones taking the flight back to lay the new eggs are not the daughters, but the granddaughters! How do they know the way back? Do I have an encoded memory from my ancestors as well?

We are imaginary beings by nature. We are continually creating stories or being wrapped up in stories; one hundred plus television channels testify to that. The world is a complicated place and we attach symbols to everything to make meaning.

This is what I believe is the real meaning behind the story of the Garden of Eden.

I began to wonder what the "moral" of the story of the Garden of Eden was compared to other stories told throughout our history and discovered that the story of Adam and Eve seemed to be the only one where punishment was eternal.

Yes, Prometheus received a horrible punishment for disobeying the gods, yet not for stealing the fire, and his punishment was not eternal, eventually he was released.

Compared to other stories, what is the moral of this story?

Morality is always aiming for the better. What was good about this story? I NOW refused to believe that I was the product of a shameful act to be eternally punished for.

I believed it was possible to see Eve as a heroine of the story, just like Prometheus was the first philanthropist of human kind.

Could Eve's disobedience actually be a gift leading to our empowerment through choice? Can there be true expression of individuality without free will to exercise it?

I now see things a bit differently than what I was led to believe.

The Garden of Eden represents the state of well-being, where nothing is missing and everything is provided for.

Everything is within reach, readily available. Yet, why would there be a tree in the middle of the garden tempting us? Why an apple?

Two simple reasons; the apple is circular and represents totality, eternity, completeness, all encompassing, infinity AND ... within the apple there is a five-pointed star and the seeded vulva—the two aspects required for creating in the physical world.

Slicing an apple horizontally (width-wise), the seed structure at the center forms a perfectly symmetrical Five-Pointed Star and slicing an apple vertically (length-wise) the core portion has the shape of the Vulva in which the Seeds are contained.

The feminine vulva shape, which contains the masculine seeds, represents the act of creation in the physical realm. Life in physical form on earth is only possible when the masculine seed enters the feminine vulva.

The seeded vulva symbolizes the complimentary aspects of duality which, when joined together, become a Union of Duality. They create life not only in the physical but also the mental realm; the two realms in the present human experience.

Why the five pointed star in the apple? The shape of the human body resembles the five-pointed star contained within a circle. The number Five represents the seen and unseen forces—matter is comprised of four elements available; fire, earth, air and water, and the quintessential fifth element which is referred to by Alchemists as Aether (breath/spirit), by the Chinese as chi, by Indian mystics as prana, or by the ancient Egyptians as Ka.

Pythagoras and his follower's secret symbol was the five-pointed star as well.

Combining all the symbols we can reach the understanding that within the circular confines of the apple exist the two aspects necessary for creation in the realm of matter; the male and female human body breathing the life force.

A male form contains the seed, while the female form is the vessel or container receiving the seed. Both are indispensable to creating life as we know it.

Both forces at once, the visible and invisible, matter and spirit, mental and emotional woven together like a spinning wheel or loom: two threads, one thread representing the spiritual (breath of life) and the other thread representing the material or physical.

The union of two threads into one magical and mysterious acts create ONE fully functioning human being that exists in two dimensions simultaneously. A seed needs a hand to plant it and the soil to germinate it, both principles, male and female, working together.

The biblical story speaks of two trees. One is the Tree of Life, and the other is the Tree of Knowledge which is of good and evil with the tree symbolizing the duality experience on earth; our exposure to two extremes or opposites constantly playing each other out, represented by the number two.

The fruit of this tree therefore is not ready or complete meaning the fruit *or what nurtures you from this source is not the truth*, because the truth is without corruption.

Truth is absolute. It is pure meaning free of contradictions, it simply IS.

Experiencing life is incomplete, because it is bound by time and space continually changing.

The Tree of Life is the Tree of Spiritual Life, or the "Tree of Unity". Unity, of course, is "one"; and "one" is the number, which is symbolic of the spiritual, united and undivided realm.

The Tree of Life, therefore, exists in the Spiritual Garden, or Spiritual womb, where all souls are prior to manifestation, or Incarnation, into the realm of matter. It is the breath itself.

Within the branches of the Tree of Knowledge of Good and Evil, the serpent entwines itself around the trunk symbolizing eternal vigilance. This particular Tree of Knowledge is deeply rooted in the concepts of duality rule by its extremes.

Our brain is only capable of seeing the world from one perspective or another until we discover and comprehend otherwise. Currently it cannot see both simultaneously. It only sees opposites like black or white, good or bad, right or wrong. Thus it has great difficulty perceiving wholeness.

Through the tree trunk, the serpent slithers with hypnotic spell-binding movements. Its wavy movements are symbolic of the shape of rivers, and the movement of water is symbolic of the flow of time, just like our thoughts running through our mind. Relentlessly, one after another we must stay vigilant. The snake symbolizes wisdom from the earth; knowledge.

Death is necessary in order to "birth" a new consciousness, a new perspective. The venom of a snake usually causes the death necessary for the old to die in order for the new to be brought in a full circle when the same venom is used to create the serum to save life—a *shift in perspective under a new light.*

Was Eve simply falling for a simple thought, doubting her worthiness? Or was it a deliberate choice to disobey in order to exercise her free will, no matter what the consequences? Was hers a deliberate act to exemplify the ultimate self-sacrifice, to be punished eternally yet to cement our individuality in the world? What would have happened if she had complied? She is the mother of all living beings, without her there would be no life because without the choice we would become lost.

Without our ability to preserve that individuality, there is no more expansion and we simply become a robot who is not meant to comply.

Eve faced the consequences of an angry male god, the ruling of a world of men, and got punished for such act. The act of disobedience was not the cause of the fall, but Eve's blame on the serpent. This act disempowered her right of choice, leading to her victimization.

Eve's fall was not claiming her free will, her right of choice, free will and taking full ownership and responsibility for her action.

A test is simply a testament to who and what we are. The eating of the apple from the Tree of Knowledge of Good and evil testifies that she forgot who she really was and believed whom she thought who she was.

By choosing to eat the apple it is a testament of our beliefs. If I do this I will be accepted, if I do that I will have this, if I say this I will be happy. The thought that separates us believes the "IF."

Continuing to transfer our ancestors' belief system, the one that speaks of us being the product of a shameful act creates a deep wound in our psyche. Setting in motion being pulled to by the extremes and living a life in disharmony.

How can we feel harmonious when we have the deep seeded belief we are born shameful and are not worthy? I entered the labyrinth of the mind to face the truth and found out that I was both; human and beast, dark and light, good and bad. By seeing I was all, I understood.

Becoming whole only meant I could not judge because there cannot be judgment in completeness. I have always been complete; nothing was missing.

The test was simple: Would I believe the thought that whispers in my mind: "I am not one with God, with the life force, one with the universe."

The gift of Eve is the right to choose because by the power of choice we are liberated. We choose to eat from the tree of life and accept life in its own terms, or we choose to believe that we are powerless in a world our limited life experience perceives as everything there is.

Do we choose to come to our center, our true knowledge of who we really are? Do we choose to honor our unique beautiful individual expression of All That Is? Or are we persuaded by each thought of doubt, questioning, continually contradicting and sending us spiraling down the rabbit hole?

Eve's choice to go against God and face punishment leads the way of being brave and having strength to move away from those merciless thoughts in our brain, that we are not good enough, that we are unworthy, that we are not the perfect creation of a benevolent and amazing universe. Such thoughts are what takes us out of the Garden of Wellness.

We can choose to not allow outside circumstances to deter us from experiencing the true essence of our being. We can pursue our deepest inner desires without the outside forces stopping us in our experiences on earth. However painful that may be at times, it is not without purpose.

The test. The apple was simple a testament of who we are. We are continually tested by opposite forces. The tree of life is connected to the earth and free to express openly.

The tree is deeply rooted and open to the sky, fully available to all. We choose the apple from that tree and we know we disconnect from the essence of who and what we are. Yet, we can make another choice to bring us back, the choice is always ours.

The word 'sin' was a term used in the Middle Ages to mean or denote missing the mark. Yet I see that "sin" originates at the moment of judgment as it creates the separation from the totality of who we really are.

Judgment is derived from opposites, like a pendulum swings back and forth. The moment this occurs, the brain cannot help but to overcompensate its position. If I think I am bad, then I will place all my efforts to do things that make me "good."

Our brain works in reverse. Instead of focusing my efforts on simply switching efforts to perform activities that demonstrate I am "good." the brain spins and creates situations that continue to prove I am "bad. "It is a spinning cycle.

Entering this mind game and believing the "IF" I am so perfect and so great like God, why is it that my life is a living hell? It's because believing the IF is the issue leading us to our suffering as it separates us at our core.

Eve believed the snake-that if she ate the apple she would be like God. She was already created in God's image. Eve, as such was complete already: nothing was missing.

By placing our trust on the definitions, we have concluded, on who or what "we think" are, we enter into judgment which separates us and bring us into extremes.

We end up being pulled by two extremes. I am good if I do this, I am bad if I do that. I am happy when I attain this, and unhappy when that is missing, etc. Being smashed against the emotional forces of our own conclusions based on what we have experienced and seeing others do or not do.

Once there we usually find overcompensating that which opposes us. Judgment occurs between two extremes while discernment includes the variables and opts for the best viable solution possible; it is solution oriented.

The two trees reflect the two poles we draw conclusions from: Life or Knowledge. Life has cycles and seasons, birth and death, while knowledge is the gathering of data rather than from our cause and consequence from our cultural experiences through life.

Eve chose the Apple that represented her wholeness from the tree of Knowledge of good and evil (corrupted). Her wholeness depended upon what she knew to be true. Based on knowledge she deviated from the truth. She saw the apple, the shinning apple in the database defining her as who she is.

She wanted to be like God, yet she was God already. How can you be that which you already are? Yes, the warning of death is real, she will get lost in the lie of what she is not, by believing that she is what she is not. The death is the disconnection from life itself.

Her choice of eating from the Tree of Knowledge of Good and evil is the equivalent of a corrupted file in the system causing the main computer to freeze or not work properly.

The moral of the story is that when we choose to believe the stories defining us as limited beings, shaming us, keeping us living in fear, in worry, we disconnect ourselves from our energy life source, our heart.

By choosing to believe that the earth plane is all that is we die because that thought is limited in itself. The expulsion from the garden was not a punishment, but a choice of deriving existence from knowledge instead of understanding. Our brain has knowledge while our heart understands because it senses life from a much broader perspective.

Adam and Eve were given the free will to choose while in the garden of wellbeing, the heart. They were born free. Eve simply exercised that choice. The good news is that her act of disobedience, just like Prometheus' act, helped everyone by cementing our right of individuality and with it, the decision to choose.

The choice lies in accepting life in its own terms where nothing is permanent and where pain is part of life. By resisting what is keeping us stuck in a vicious circle of continually trying to change or fix and never accomplishing it. The choice of trading the heart for the brain only leads to our suffering; and instead of moving into expansion, we stall.

Life is expansion in itself, movement as the transforming and creating impulse. Spirit is simply every breath, in an out, marking the perfect flow, the ever present moment continually moving and changing and us flowing with it.

The truth is that there are two forces playing against each other at all times. The density of the earth physicality can be at times overwhelming given that our sensibilities are finely tuned to previous experience of pain, disappointment, confusion, or depression.

We have gotten lost in a world of intellect dominated by the mind and it will be our decision to get back to the truth of our being, to our core.

This will not be easy because it requires extreme measures like the decision to disconnect from the outside information sources that continue bombarding us; stopping the news, the radio, the internet so we create a space where our own inner voice can be heard. How can we discern that *'quiet still voice'* in a world of constant accelerated stimuli?

By exercising our power of choice we can again enter the garden of well-being. If one thought changes our direction, in the same way another thought can bring us back into our well-being if we so choose.

A house divided cannot stand; we hear Lincoln's voice with resounding truth that *as long as we are split within ourselves, the suffering will continue*.

Structure of the mind must collapse. Strong foundations at the core of our being solidify our strength even though the so-called "evidence" or facts say otherwise.

Our choices determine our actions.
Our actions define our character...
Our character determines our destiny...

Darth Vader in Stars Wars.

RETURN OF THE KING

By Sir Thomas Malory

Once upon, Igraine, the wife of the Duke of Cornwall, smites King Uther Pendragon. Disguising himself as Igraine's husband he sneaks into her bed and she conceives Arthur.

Merlin the wizard raises Arthur away from his parents. It is Merlin who had designed for Arthur's father Uther a great Round Table at which 150 knights could sit. Upon Uther's death, the knights do not know who should take his place. Merlin tells them that whoever could draw a mysterious sword out of a stone should be the next king. Many try but all fail. Then one day Arthur, who is attending his foster brother Sir Kay, is sent to find a sword to replace his brother's broken one. He comes upon the magical sword Excalibur in the stone and, not knowing the prophecy, drew it out. Thus, he is proclaimed the new king.

Arthur unites the thorn kingdom and becomes a benevolent and well-loved king. His reign is known for its heroic deeds and chivalric romance and the name of his castle, Camelot, signify a golden age.

Until one day, King Arthur had gone far across the sea, for he loved his own country so well, that to gain glory at home made him happiest of all.

But a false knight with his followers was laying waste the country across the sea, and Arthur had gone to wage war against him.

'And you, Sir Modred, will rule the country while I am gone,' the King had said. And the knight smiled as he thought of the power that would be his.

At first the people missed their great King Arthur, but as the months passed they began to forget him, and to talk only of Sir Modred and his ways.

And he, that he might gain the people's praise, made easier laws than ever Arthur had done, till by and by there were many in the country who wished that the King would never come back.

When Modred knew what the people wished, he was glad, and he made up his mind to do a cruel deed. He would cause letters to be written from beyond the sea, and the letters would tell that the great King Arthur had been slain in battle. And when the letters came the people read, 'King Arthur is dead,' and they believed the news was true.

And there were some who wept because the noble King was slain, but some had no time to weep. 'We must find a new King,' they said. And because his laws were easy, these chose Sir Modred to rule over them.

The wicked knight was pleased that the people wished him to be their King. 'They shall take me to Canterbury to crown me,' he said proudly. And the nobles took him there, and amid shouts and rejoicings he was crowned.

But it was not very long till other letters came from across the sea, saying that King Arthur had not been slain, and that he was coming back to rule over his own country once more.

When Sir Modred heard that King Arthur was on his way home, he collected a great army and went to Dover to try to keep the King from landing. But no army would have been strong enough to keep Arthur and his knights away from the country they loved so well. They fought fiercely till they got on shore and scattered all Sir Modred's men. Then the knight gathered together another army, and chose a new battle-field. But King Arthur fought so bravely that he and his men were again victorious, and Sir Modred fled to Canterbury.

Many of the people began to forsake the false knight now, and saying that he was a traitor, they went back to King Arthur.

But still Sir Modred wished to conquer the King. He would go through the counties of Kent and Surrey and raise a new army.

Now King Arthur had dreamed that if he fought with Sir Modred again he would be slain. So when he heard that the knight had raised another army, he thought, 'I will meet this traitor who has betrayed me. When he looks in my face, he will be ashamed and remember his vow of obedience.'

And he sent two bishops to Sir Modred. 'Say to the knight that the King would speak with him alone,' said Arthur. And the traitor thought, 'The King wishes to give me gold or great power, if I send my army away without fighting.' 'I will meet King Arthur,' he said to the bishops. But because he did not altogether trust the King he said he would take fourteen men with him to the meeting-place, 'and the King must have fourteen men with him too,' said Sir Modred. 'And our armies shall keep watch when we meet, and if a sword is lifted it shall be the signal for battle.'

Then King Arthur arranged a feast for Sir Modred and his men. And as they feasted all went merrily till an adder glided out of a little bush and stung one of the knight's men. And the pain was so great, that the man quickly drew his sword to kill the adder.

And when the armies saw the sword flash in the light, they sprang to their feet and began to fight, 'for this is the signal for battle,' they thought. And when evening came there were many thousand slain and wounded, and Sir Modred was left alone. But Arthur had still two knights with him, Sir Lucan and Sir Bedivere.

When King Arthur saw that his army was lost and all his knights slain but two, he said, 'Would to God I could find Sir Modred, who has caused all this trouble.'

'He is yonder,' said Sir Lucan, 'but remember your dream, and go not near him.'

'Whether I die or live,' said the King, 'he shall not escape.' And seizing his spear he ran to Sir Modred, crying, 'Now you shall die.'

And Arthur smote him under the shield, and the spear passed through his body, and he died. Then, wounded and exhausted, the King fainted, and his knights lifted him and took him to a little chapel not far from a lake. As the King lay there, he heard cries of fear and pain from the distant battle-field.

'What causes these cries?' said the King wearily. And to soothe the sick King, Sir Lucan said he would go to see. And when he reached the battle-field, he saw in the moonlight that robbers were on the field stooping over the slain, and taking from them their rings and their gold. And those that were only wounded, the robbers slew, that they might take their jewels too.

Sir Lucan hastened back, and told the King what he had seen.

'We will carry you farther off, lest the robbers find us here,' said the knights. And Sir Lucan lifted the King on one side and Sir Bedivere lifted him on the other.

But Sir Lucan had been wounded in the battle, and as he lifted the King he fell back and died.

Then Arthur and Sir Bedivere wept for the fallen knight.

Now the King felt so ill that he thought he would not live much longer, and he turned to Sir Bedivere: 'Take Excalibur, my good sword,' he said, 'and go with it to the lake, and throw it into its waters. Then come quickly and tell me what you see.'

Sir Bedivere took the sword and went down to the lake. But as he looked at the handle with its sparkling gems and the richness of the sword, he thought he could not throw it away. 'I will hide it carefully here among the rushes,' thought the knight. And when he had hidden it, he went slowly to the King and told him he had thrown the sword into the lake.

'What did you see?' asked the King eagerly.

'Nothing but the ripple of the waves as they broke on the beach,' said Sir Bedivere.

'You have not told me the truth,' said the King. 'If you love me, go again to the lake, and throw my sword into the water.'

Again the knight went to the water's edge. He drew the sword from its hiding-place. He would do the King's will, for he loved him. But again the beauty of the sword made him pause. 'It is a noble sword; I will not throw it away,' he murmured, as once more he hid it among the rushes. Then he went back more slowly, and told the King that he had done his will.

'What did you see?' asked the King.

'Nothing but the ripples of the waves as they broke on the beach,' repeated the knight.

'You have betrayed me twice,' said the King sadly, 'and yet you are a noble knight! Go again to the lake, and do not betray me for a rich sword.'

Then for the third time Sir Bedivere went to the water's edge, and drawing the sword from among the rushes, he flung it as far as he could into the lake.

And as the knight watched, an arm and a hand appeared above the surface of the lake. He saw the hand seize the sword, and shaking it three times, disappear again under the water. Then Sir Bedivere went back quickly to the King, and told him what he had seen.

'Carry me to the lake,' entreated Arthur, 'for I have been here too long. And the knight carried the King on his shoulders down to the water's side. There they found a barge lying, and seated in it were three Queens, and each Queen wore a black hood. And when they saw King Arthur they wept.

'Lay me in the barge,' said the King. And when Sir Bedivere had laid him there, King Arthur rested his head on the lap of the fairest Queen. And they rowed from land.

Sir Bedivere, left alone, watched the barge as it drifted out of sight, and then he went sorrowfully on his way, till he reached a hermitage. And he lived there as a hermit for the rest of his life.

And the barge was rowed to a vale where the King was healed of his wound.

And some say that now he is dead, but others say that King Arthur will come again, and clear the country of its foes.

Chapter XIII

THE PEACEMAKER

There is a candle in your heart, ready to be kindled.
There is a void in your soul, ready to be filled.
You feel it, don't you?
–Rumi

Our brain is the ultimate supercomputer, making us the finest human processor engineered by the universe. Our senses resemble highly sensitive tentacles. We observe and replicate what our caregivers do, extremely well. We love stories and become ourselves great storytellers. We have shown incredible adaptability and we practice it masterfully.

There is no doubt whatsoever of how brilliant we are, just look around to see how far we have come in just one hundred years. I do not need to tell you that not long ago we were just riding buggies pulled by horses and now we fly jets.

So if we are so incredible smart why is it that we cannot figure out something as simple as the delivery of food to the people starving in Africa? We have gone to the moon, we have super-fast cars and computers and yet we cannot figure out simple food distribution? Why do we continue fighting war after war? I believe that it is simply because the old software of lack and fear continues to play in the background.

Fear was instilled in us long ago and it looks like it is continuing to run us, literally. An image is worth a thousand words...

I believe that the reason why seems to be that we are stuck in what seems to be a split: extremely smart in some ways and extremely stupid in others, especially in regards to emotions.

It is widely known that media uses techniques to persuade us, how organized religion contradicts its dogma,
and still, we continue to live in contradictions. Our life is a contradiction.

In Luke 14:26 Jesus speaks: "If anyone comes to me and does not hate father and mother, wife and children, brothers and sisters--yes even their own life--such person cannot be my disciple."

Was this an invitation to disregard all the stories implanted, to break tradition? Yet, I wanted to be part of the group, I wanted to participate, to collaborate and found myself always at odds and always compromising my needs.

What this is suggesting is that in order to find your true essence, and be truly free and unconditioned beings, we must walk away from the legacy of our elders.

It was obvious that within the group there was no room for individual expression, it was all about the safe-keeping of the rules ensuring the survival of the group itself.

So, what if instead of continuing the legacy of suffering and punishment, I opened to the wellness of my being that was within, already.

What if the stories could be deleted just like files in the computer? What if the story was treated like a virus in the system preventing me from "running" efficiently? From having a happy fulfilling life?

Chapter XIV

ROUND TABLE

Be grateful for whoever comes, because each
has been sent as a guide from beyond.
-Rumi

There were so many voices in my head, as if I had an angry mob at my door. The more I refused to disregard them, the louder they got. The stronger was the voice of safety and security, insisting that I was not safe. Some voices screamed "danger" and others "freedom" while others judged me and accused me, shamed me, threatened me.

With my willing Heart to hear all the voices, I used every uncomfortable experience as an opportunity to clear conditioning and programming. When something would irritate me or frustrate me, I would "turn the other cheek" which to me meant to turn the view towards me, 180 degrees.

Was the experience mirroring something within me? When I started to look at situations from a mirror perspective every situation was leverage to delete corrupted files distorting my view.

Instead of pointing the finger in an accusative manner, I simply asked the question: that person is expressing anger towards me and I feel this reactiveness boiling within me, is that situation reflecting anger within me?

A quest is simply a question and I got into the habit of asking questions instead of immediately jumping into conclusions or worse, judgments. Every time I thought I was are so sure we know all the answers. I was proven wrong over and over.

My usual attitude was to react angrily towards situations that angered me. So instead of projecting with my usual yelling frustration, I saw it as a call to dive in deeply, with a grateful attitude for what was happening. I did not understand, yet I trusted that there was a gift in it. The situation was mirroring something hidden that was ready to be reconciled, to clear the way to the true part of my being.

To me, turning the other cheek meant changing the position from which I was looking at my experience. I have repeatedly told my girls that instead of pointing your finger at others in accusation, turn it 180 degrees toward you; this is a good practice.

Was Jesus an invitation to turn our head in the direction of the hit? To investigate was a call to explore all the parts that have been hidden because when we do, we are changing the position where we are coming from, and with it our perspective.

Seeing whatever it is in others and judging it, we are called to change our perspective and as it changes, so does our perception.

When something that we dislike is calling our attention, and we feel the anger boiling up, the frustration rises.

The tendency, given our training learned from our caregiver, is to suppress it. So our need is to take a look at it. If we notice the human body design, our view is 180 degrees; we do not see everything; especially behind our back where obviously, there are no eyes.

So by turning the other cheek, we are able to grasp a full view of the surroundings and our perspective is broader. When we go about making assumptions, like the popular saying goes: when you assume, you make an ass of you and me.

This is what I experienced when I started turning my cheek towards the disliked reaction caused within me. I simply took a look at it without judgment, just with an honest desire to see the truth.

Soon I realized that everything was related and deeply connected to those hidden parts. By turning my attention toward them, I could simply bring them to light and they would almost instantly disappear.

I remember complaining about the father of my children being a control freak, and soon realized that I was a control freak myself. My immediate reaction was, of course, to deny it: "Oh no, I am not." I would scream. The bigger the resistance, the clearer was the mirror.

By practicing soon it became clear that the world was mirroring all those suppressed parts of self. I experienced angry people snapping at me, pushing me, abusing me. And each time, when I would go deep into core to explore it, sure enough I was doing that to myself!

How could I not? All I observed others doing was to abuse me and abuse others, I learned well. I had been a master at adaptation. Because I allowed others to keep me caged, I caged myself. Because I allowed others to abuse me, I abused myself.

The gift of the mirror was now an opportunity to look at everything, and use it to my advantage, to liberate the caged self.

Also, to listen, really listen to what the voices had to say - and little by little, after they have been acknowledged - they began to quiet down.

King Arthur sits not at the head of the table. *The king, the Heart,* stands in no fixed position. Heart considers everything, listens to everything, and after considering all the input received from all his knights, his close advisors of wisdom (intelligence) and intellect (brain) and the king (heart) would lead the way.

True leadership considers everything with a kind and compassionate heart. With a deep appreciation for everyone's services, acknowledges everyone.

The knight responsible for security and safety within the kingdom is fully focused on this only. That is his duty.

Likewise the knight responsible for ensuring self-expression within the kingdom has no other concern other than making sure personal freedoms are not infringed upon. Each has a voice in the round table, and together contributes to the kingdom wellbeing.

The importance of a king, a magnanimous Heart within the kingdom becomes essential because it gathers all the forces and weaves them to create expansion and well-being.

The willingness to simply move toward the Heart and engage the brain in a collaborative and supportive role is courage. To simply listen to what the voices have to say without hastily making conclusions is a heart function.

The heart is interested in solutions. It trades righteousness for functionality, for what works. No blame, no shame, no judgment.

Decisions when made with an open heart are perfectly aligned and harmonious. A brain without a heart becomes a tyrant, a heart without a head is pitiful and hands without both are useless.

Chapter XV

HOLY GRAIL

Everything in the universe is within you.
Ask all from yourself
-Rumi

Through the power of choice we define our character. Choice is what confirms our individuality and the core of who we really are. We at some point must stop blaming the world and ourselves for our experience.

By choice, our free will, we truly delineate our destiny. Yes, I know it is hard. I walk the road of duality each day; I know it is not easy, yet I know it is possible.

At some point in our lives we are called to take the journey. In his story Theseus chose to enter the labyrinth and face the Minotaur, find the truth and set it free.

Remember that we create stories, believe them and then get stuck in them. The truth is that nothing is missing and everything is all-inclusive in our lives; we all have a role to play in our movie. We choose to take each breath, being fully present with reality, to BE what we are, the cosmos itself.

Choosing to believe our story, that we are worthless and sinful, leads to a condition of constant suffering and heartache.

Yet, a different choice can liberate us. How? By choosing to be in the moment, fully present and therein - to fully acknowledge that the conditioning and programming of the group must be deleted.

To walk alone is a lonely road yet we must if we are to be free. A choice to turn towards the pain we experience is a choice of valor and compassion toward ourselves, an act of bravery.

Camelot, our heart, is at the core of our being waiting for us to accept the beast we have created and stop rejecting, to love unconditionally and without judgment.

We are both the dark and the light, the good and the bad, the hero/heroine; or the coward or villain/victim, the beautiful or the ugly, the All encompassed in one instrument: our human body.

A choice to move toward our hearts and away from our brain is a smart move because it is only within our hearts that we will re-discover and re-member who we really are.

What if this Garden of Eden is right here, right now? And the only requirement is for us to be vigilant and not fall asleep amidst all the thoughts badgering us constantly.

What if we have never left and there is nowhere to go? What if within us remains the choice to listen to the voice speaking the truth - instead of the ones insisting we are the product of shame, and what we must do in order to attain?

When I stopped looking to the outside world for answers, and turned my accusatory finger 180 degrees towards me, I found myself in the habit of judging others and myself very harshly. That was a major discovery.

By constantly focusing my attention on what the world was mirroring about me, I stopped myself in my tracks. I learned to intently work to re-train the thought patterns continually playing in my brain. When judgment appeared, I switched immediately, to say to self: *I don't know*, instead of making an assumption or jumping to conclusions.

I replaced habitual worry with a simple acknowledgment of "I guess we are going to find out." Every invading thought that insisted on putting me down, or telling me I wouldn't get what I desired; I changed it to: "*Maybe. Let's wait and see.*"

I connected with nature as much as possible - alone and without any kind of external interruptions. Somewhere, deep within me, there was a voice that was not being heard. So, realizing that, I started setting up a time of 5 or 10 minutes to just observe.

I listened, really listened to the ideas, thoughts and voices that popped in my head. They seemed to be due to the bombarding of external stimuli activating self-talk and on-going reactions. So with a kind heart and an inquisitive mind, I asked to be told more.

That meant a willingness to stay with whatever arose and notice how the images, memories, and sound came up along with the feelings.

Most importantly— I learned how to connect with the feelings and thoughts which accompany these images. I learned to sit with them without an agenda as the observer, without reaction.

With that as a daily routine, I began to trust whatever occurred was what I was called to be with. I began to focus on what I had instead of what I did not. Expressing admiration for small things like running water or a flushing toilet led me to Gratitude.

Yes, as a child I had to carry water on my shoulders to wash dishes and laundry. I hated using the gross and stinky outhouse. I did laundry outside and by hand in the horrible Texas winters.

Little by little, I changed the focus and the lenses got bigger. I chose to build the new instead of fixing the old, and especially to fix myself.

Soon, I realized that Camelot had always been here, a thought away.

So in this way, I started deleting files seven years ago. It has taken a long time and I am still in the process. It is amazing how much junk I had stored in this brilliant gray blob of mind that oddly enough, looks like a labyrinth.

Chapter XVI

RESET, REBOOT, RESTART.

Close both eyes to see with the other eye.
-Rumi

It is said that our children lead us into our destiny. During the battles getting my girls back I utilized the time to discover and experience life from a different perspective

Following a friend's advice to go back to school, in 2012 I moved to Sacramento area to attend Rudolf Steiner College (RSC) to pursue a career as a Waldorf Teacher. There I experienced for the first time in my life that I was okay just the way I was; that I was not broken and that there was nothing wrong with me.

It was there that I discovered that what I thought I was, I was not! I had been what others wanted me to be. In a new environment I was able to feel supported so that I could, and did, awaken abilities and talents buried long ago.

The RSC environment for expansion was a safe container where everything was welcome and not judged. It also seemed to be the next step complementing studies as an Energy Coach; where I had learned to tune into intuitive abilities I had deeply suppressed since childhood. I explored my ideas without being punished or where my self-expression felt threatened.

By applying the curriculum and the child stages of development to myself, I had the opportunity to rapidly expand my consciousness.

As a child I had never allowed myself to be as a child, for my days were spent working to make up for what I was receiving. RSC became the opportunity of my life to simply be a child again.

Attending RSC gave me the opportunity to stand outside myself and grasp the importance of comparing and contrasting without analyzing, only through pure observation. It simply gave me the opportunity to learn how to discriminate without judging—go to opposites without getting stuck in one point of view.

That exposure to completely different points of view widened the lenses of how I perceived life and the joy to be in an environment where self-expression is welcomed and encouraged.

In the rich soil provided at RSC my abilities in reading energy and auras expanded and cemented. It was safe to practice my development of "seeing" that which was not evident to the naked human eye.

As a child I would form an image and thus make it "real" thereby giving it energy to materialize in physical form. From my child's point of view, I was worthless.

That had been reflected by my caregivers and formed my perceptions based on what I 'saw' reflected back at me.

And even though it was not true, at the time there was no one who could help me understand it differently.

Today I realize that the lack of compassion and kindness from others toward me was not a reflection of me but theirs. I internalized their inability to move beyond their own wounding.

Later, in 2013 another level of my unfolding life occurred. I had opened a private shop experimenting with a form of intuitive analysis. In counseling sessions one day I felt the very strong impulse to place my hands on the persons head, lightly, very softly.

In doing so while guiding them into a deep state of relaxation and prompting them with questions on what they "saw" with their eyes closed; they confirmed what I sensed they were "seeing."

Each client invariably and repeatedly confirmed what I would sense and somehow our connection enabled each of us to find answers inside our own self in a manner quite difficult to describe.

After many sessions with similar results with different people, I could no longer deny it. There is a place within where each person can access their interpersonal aspects and be able to alter, change or delete files or traumatic experiences.

It sounds crazy, I know. I doubted it myself. Further, case after case, I found that the person would not need help after three or fewer sessions.

Each would say that they were feeling good, and yes, life was still challenging but they felt they could handle it. They felt confident and energized.

During such counseling sessions, it became clear to me what Einstein was referring to when he said, "Imagination is more important than intelligence." Somehow, just like accessing the main frame of a supercomputer, clients were directly accessing their archived files and were able to then modify them.

As I understand the process for a client, a perceived problem or situation is solved by looking at it from the adult perspective while being fully awakened or with an open mind and utilizing imagination and attentive focus.

Counseling Session Notes:

"Imagination is more important than knowledge. Knowledge is limited. Imagination encircles the world."
– Albert Einstein

Session # 10 50 Year Old Male April 13, 2014

He and I spoke briefly about his mind racing and the paralyzing effect it was having in his life. He considered himself a man of high intelligence with a degree in Mechanics and another in Physics. He had been out of work for 3 years and it had taken its toll on him. He expressed how his brain had "given up" to what I said "great!" He was in the right place where the healing process could begin, I meant going to where the truth was.

I listened attentively getting insight of what was really going on--his fears, his worries. What was the worst that could happen "IF"? I asked. I pushed him to go down the rabbit hole. He replied: If I don't not snap out of this.... I will lose my family, I will end up sleeping on a family's couch, and I will be homeless. I will be abused.... there was an intense silence and he controlled his tears.

I believed he was sexually molested at the age of 12 while in a Catholic school. He had not realized his confession and I have not dug into it either.

I suggested we enter into this sacred space, the Heart Chakra. He agreed to do the exercise.

I led him into a state of relaxation, breathing deeper with his eyes closed. I placed my hands on his head. I felt the heat and activity going on. I guided him into following the light in the tunnel--there was lots of resistance. I waited patiently without pushing him.

I suggested him to call someone he trusted to walk with him into the tunnel and if there was no one I would go with him.

I asked him to describe the door he saw when he got to the light.

"Blue" he told me. I asked him to describe it. "Rectangular" he replied.

"Open it and go in," I said.

"Can't get it, the handle is broken" he told me (interestingly he had been unable to "handle" things all his life).

I suggested he look around for some tool so he could fix it. He does and gets in. I asked him to describe the room. He said: "it is dark."

I tell him to walk with his back against the wall and feel with his hands for some opening, a window, or drapes.

He said: "There are shutters."

I asked him to open them to let the light in.

What do you see? I asked

"A pool" he says.

His voice changes and expresses: WOW!

I ask him where he is at. "In the pool," he responds.

I suggest he enjoy it and soak in the entire well-being he was experiencing.

I asked him about the shutter. He says, “It is gone.”

Where is the light coming from? Is there a sunroof?

He said: “Yes, an opening in the ceiling.”

What do you see? “Clouds” he says.

Are you enjoying it? “Oh yes,” he said.

He was completely relaxed in a mellow state.

I asked him to describe to me the room he was in. “it is full of statues. There are lots of them. I see The David.”

I allow him to enjoy his stay in that place for about 5 minutes.

I asked if someone would bring him a beverage.

“Oh yes!” he said.

“Restore, reset, and reboot.” I said while touching the head I commanded to the brain wires [synopsis].

I told him it was time to leave, yet before you exit look for a letter, a note. He couldn’t find anything.

I prompted him to look by the David statue.

He looked for it and found a marble tablet. I told him to read it.

“Welcome.”

I told him to bring it with him when he got out and to seal the door behind him.

He opened his eyes and exclaimed" WOW, that was real." He gave me looks of "I can't believe it."

SESSION # 11 Twelve Year Old Boy April 17, 2014

I guided him to start the ocean breath and I asked permission to place my hands on his head.

Guide him into bringing a beam of light form the 4th Sun. filling up his body sitting on a hollow tree stump roots to the core of the earth. A violet light in the middle of the stump to transmute whatever comes up. An edge of white roses around him and a staff like Moses's staff where all that is not needed anymore, all the illusions will be realized.

There is a burning bush. Listen to it. When you get close to it, there is a door, describe it to me. He tells me it is a green door, regular size. I tell him to enter and seal it behind him so no one will enter. He sees only white in the room.

I ask him to find a place to sit and wait for what he needs to listen to.

He tells me an old woman is showing up.

I ask him to ask her why she is here.

He tells me she tells him: "to help you."

I prompt him to ask her how she can help you.

He says she has told him: "See clearly..."

He asks her to show him how. Silent moments...

Where is she, I asked, "Is she still there?"

Does she have something to give you?

He responds: "Courage."

I guide him to thank her and ask her to leave.

I ask him to look around. He sees white and beams of light.

I ask him to stand on the beams of light and wash off all the dark/past lives and let all go down the drain in the floor.

I ask him "how does the room look now?"

He replies: "Everything is full of color—Green, brown, blue." He likes it.

Ask him if he sees a note. Look for a piece of paper. He does not see anything like that. I ask him if there is writing on the wall...

He reads: "Be Happy."

I ask him to bow to the room, thanking the place. He gets out of the room.

SESSION # 12 40 Year old Woman April 25, 2014

Door opens into a cave where light is very dim. Something prevents her from getting to the light. When she asks if it is fear, the cave lightens up and then the walls look distorted. I suggest using dynamite to blow them up. She does and she finds herself in the bottom of the ocean. The water is filthy and it is full of trash.

She describes a big man with long beard and a trident (Poseidon). He is angry, yelling at her and she does not understand what he says. She asks how she can help. He points to her to clean up the mess. She does. Then the ocean is clean and again she finds herself on the shore.

I asked her if there is a bird flying by? She says: There was one just before you said it. A seagull just flew by above my head on the left side.

I ask her to check in the seagull's leg for a note. She retrieves it and it reads: "I was here."

What does it mean, she asks? I said.... you were there; this is your home, your origins. She replies with a confirming "oh, I see..."

She turns around and sees a house in the distance. She goes to it and thinks about entering, yet half of the house is in darkness and the other half has light. She describes it like a long stable where the horses are kept. The right side is in complete darkness and the side on the left has light in the end...

She walks throughout this stable like building to get to the room with the light. In the room there is pasture and a horse is lying down in the middle, he is sick and breathing heavily, like out of breath. "He is dying," she says.

I prompt her to go to him and ask how she can help. The horse tells her to bandage his legs. I guide her to place her hand on his heart and breathe with him. He gets better. They get out of the stable into the sandy beach.

I guide her to put the whole house in a bubble and fill the bubble with golden light.

Put another bubble next to it, a twelve inch golden filter between the two bubbles. Pass the bubble with the house in through the filter into the second bubble. As she does, the darkness and the house surrounding it disappear like smoke. Then the new bubble expands into the whole area bringing more light into it all.

Still... she notices darkness in the other side. I ask her to fill a bucket with golden light and paint it all with a big brush. Now it looks nice and bright again. Yet, the sky seems to have dark clouds and she does not like it. I tell her that dark clouds are part of the landscape. Some days are rainy, others sunny. She seems to agree. I ask her to follow a road where she will find a door and before she exits she will bow to the sacred place and give thanks. She exits and goes up a ladder.

At the end of the session I asked her to pick one of my angel cards.

The card she pulled out of the deck: VULNERABILITY. Understanding duality. She was having difficulty accepting the darkness. Resisting the ugly. Wanted only "perfection." I tell her the lotus grows in filthy waters; there can't be light without the dark. Any piece of art has a background; contrast is part of the painting. I show her the face of a lady in the picture at my altar where the dark background delineates her beautiful face.

SESSION # 13 - Seven-Year-Old Boy June 5, 2014

Sitting by the kitchen table with my girls, he started telling us that there were people dancing on top of the trees. I asked him questions of who they were, why they were there, how many. I placed my hands on his head and guided him into disposing of them. They fought him back, slamming him on the wall, cutting hands, meeting the devil, there is a gate in heaven, and there is hell I must go to find the devil.

At the end of the session he breathed a sigh of relief. He expressed how "they" were on him; trying to get his body and they were not letting him concentrate at school. He was glad they were gone.

Spoke with his mom afterwards and she said that sometime she got the impression that he was not acting his age, as if it was not he.

The child expressed to my girls that "only hands of steel could open his scalp made of metal."

SESSION # 14 - 60 Year Old Lady July 3, 2014

Situation: Debate over right and wrong about abortion righteousness.

Person continues to say over and over "I want to be clean."

She had spoken with two priests and they told her no reason to tell her lover about three previous terminations. She had "confessed" and she was now "clean."

She was sorry and that was it. "But you are not sorry" I said to her.

"Yes, I am." She expressed that when she did it, a while ago, she had no doubt at all... it was a matter of fact.

I notice the continual conflict between religion and spirituality. She does not believe it is wrong to terminate the pregnancies, yet, she wants to be clean.

I continued to probe with more questions. Very confused. What is the root of this dilemma? Mentally she is very strong.

When I say affirmatively: You believe in abortion.

She reacts angrily and tells me: "BELIEVE??? How can you believe?" She raises her voice at me frustrated as if I am judging her.

Back and forth, she insists and I am able to see that she justifies it. In her mind it is okay now she has done it in the past, yet she won't approve it is "right". And yet, she will support women through it.

She tells me that after getting clearance from the priests this morning, she is "clean." She did not even need to come to see me.

"I said, okay, would you do an exercise with me?"

While we use tapping I asked her to repeat after me:

"I am clean, I am so clean. Everything is clean within me." She almost jumps with joy. She feels great. We continue tapping.

"I am so clean." "Not even a scratch within me..." She slows down, doubts continuing tapping. "Well, there is a small one in my heart." We stop. She feels sad.

I suggested to her to invite the three souls that would have inhabited the bodies she terminated. She jumped to the idea.

I led her into the light, and she describes the door being a regular and color red.

She walks in. It is a garden setting. She sits and asks the first soul to come; it is a boy. He looks sad. Why? Because he wanted to have a wonderful mother and he was not able to. She apologetically explained to him that she terminated the pregnancy, because she was young and immature, she was not ready. Her sadness finally comes out. I suggested she ask him if she would have chosen to have him, would he have had that experience. He said "No because you were not ready." He starts to fade. I told her to ask him to go to the light and thank him.

The second soul is invited, it is a boy. He looks like he does not know what she is talking about, as if she speaks Chinese. The termination was not an issue to him. Being pregnant was only an opportunity for him to have a human experience, yet it did not work out, oh well... next time. She leads him to the light and thanks him.

The third soul is a girl. She explains again to this soul the reason why she did it, why she terminated the pregnancy. The girl understands. She wishes the girl would have a beautiful family.

I ask her to ask the girl if she has had that experience, yet. The girl tell her that she has been born into a wonderful family. Lady is happy and relieved.

End of session, she realizes all the sadness repressed and not being able to expressed it freely. She feels thrilled, happy, relieved. All is well.

SESSION # 15 - 30 Year Old Lady - November 7, 2014

The theme of the day was: the Tear of the Self happened and willingness to go in and mend the bond. She was willing, yet terrified.

I sensed there would be a lot of resistance so I made sure to place the 'no disturb' sign at my front gate, locked all doors and disconnected phone to prevent distractions.

We went in, everything was completely dark. I asked to take the golden yard in her hand so she could find her way out. I told her I had walked this terrain many times and that I was with her. It felt like a labyrinth with brick walls and rough dirt road, bumpy. I assured her the yard would help us get back.

She was about to describe the door when something dropped on the floor in the direction of the kitchen. It sounded as if a bomb had dropped. We both jumped at the sound and trembled. I kept my hands on her hand and guided her to close her eyes again and not worry. I stayed grounded even though the blood in my whole body and my heart were racing.

I guided her in... She describes the door as a heart shape with three holes stacked up in a line; one on top, on the middle and one at the bottom. Light is filtering through the holes of the door. It is an old rustic door with a rusted knob. She enters and describes an office, a plain office.

She says that it is quite big, about 4 x 8. She giggles nervously at the thought of burning it because it will set the whole office on fire. I tell her why not? You do not care for that place anyway, do you? I asked. She does it and tells me the whole office is burning down.

I asked her where she was at now. She describes a beautiful place, a meadow surrounded by a forest. She feels wonderful here, she feels happy. I invite her to soak it in. then she says, "Wait, should not my children be here?" "Not really, no 'should,' " I said. I tell her that they can join her and she can be with them, she does and they come in. I suggest that they go back to their space and she can invite them another time. Your children are a part of you always with you; you are their mother, yet they have their own journey. It is like a dance, they come and they go.

The children go back into the forest and I ask her if there is a road, a sign of some sort for her to follow. She said, there is an arrow pointing up stairs. I invite her to follow it. She climbs up the stairs and gets to see the whole place from high above. She feels great. She describes it like the hills in Scotland. I lead her out after integrating it all in her system. She gives thanks to the place and walks out the door. I tell her to follow the golden yarn.

She looks very peaceful.

I place on her lap the item that had fallen startling us at the beginning of the session... a picture of a blue butterfly with letters at the bottom: TRANSFORM.

She burst into tears. It has been four sessions, she has kept her wits all the way, being strong and not expressing her sadness. She has been pushing all the emotions down until finally she lets go.

"TEAR DOWN THE STRUCTURE"

There is nothing that brings more joy during my counseling sessions than to see a human go back to the pure and true essence of being.

There is a way to use imagination to get to our core. The same monsters imagined can be imagined away. The tool used to create beliefs about beasts burning in hell, encoding our mapping of the world as we know it, can *be used* to reinstate us back to our original state, our virginal state; which simply means free of contradictions. Our brain encompasses all that data assimilated during lifetimes and passed down through our DNA. If it was filed there, it can be deleted the same way.

Hope remains in a world of chaos, faithfully waiting for us to make the call.

Your choice...

www.ingramcontent.com/pod-product-compliance
Lightning Source LLC
LaVergne TN
LVHW010619100826
845148LV00014B/3037

* 9 7 8 0 6 9 2 3 6 8 4 4 2 *